When Jesus Prays Through You

RELEASE THE INFINITE POWER OF HEAVEN IN YOUR LIFE

by

Charles Capps

HARRISON HOUSE
Tulsa, Oklahoma

08 07 06 05   10 9 8 7 6 5 4 3 2 1

When Jesus Prays Through You:
Release the Infinite Power of Heaven in Your Life
ISBN 1-57794-733-9
(Previously published as ISBN 0-89274-853-2, *Jesus Our Intercessor*)
Copyright ©1994 by Charles Capps
P.O. Box 69
England, Arkansas 72046

Published by Harrison House, Inc.
P.O. Box 35035
Tulsa, Oklahoma 74153

Contents

Introduction

We have all been taught about Jesus and His healing ministry, working miracles, and casting out demons. But the Church (the Body of Christ) as a whole knows very little about Jesus as our Intercessor. This part of His ministry is so vital to us; it is not only something He did when He lived on earth, but it is a continuing ministry today.

This book will take you on a scriptural journey that will shed light on many truths you already know. Be sensitive to what God says to you as you read this book and study God's Word.

1

There Was No Intercessor

1

There Was No Intercessor

There have been many questions and much confusion over some things that happened to God's people under the Old Covenant. Many today try to link things that were suffered then to what we can expect to experience. But God has provided better things for us. (Heb. 11:40.)

First, let's look at some of the reasons why the people of the Old Covenant suffered things that we should not have to suffer today.

In the book of Ecclesiastes, Solomon gives us his view of the situation under the Old Covenant:

> **So I returned, and considered all the oppressions that are done under the sun: and behold the tears of such as were oppressed, and they had no comforter; and on the side of their oppressors there was power; but they had no comforter.**
>
> **Wherefore I praised the dead which are already dead more than the living which are yet alive.**

Yea, better is he than both they, which hath not yet been, who hath not seen the evil work that is done under the sun.

Ecclesiastes 4:1-3

In that day the oppressed had no comforter, but there was power on the side of the oppressor. Solomon praised the dead rather than the living. In other words, it was his opinion that they would be better off dead than to live under their condition.

Isaiah states:

And judgment is turned away backward, and justice standeth afar off: for truth is fallen in the street, and equity cannot enter.

Yea, truth faileth; and he that departeth from evil maketh himself a prey: and the Lord saw it, and it displeased him that there was no judgment.

And he saw that there was no man, and wondered that *there was no intercessor:* therefore his arm brought salvation unto him; and his right-eousness, it sustained him.

Isaiah 59:14-16

Here we find the key to why many things happened under the Old Covenant that should never happen to us today: *they had no intercessor.*

God speaks through Ezekiel:

The people of the land have used oppression, and exercised robbery, and have vexed the poor and needy: yea, they have oppressed the stranger wrongfully.

And *I sought for a man* among them, that should make up the hedge, and stand in the gap before me for the land, that I should not destroy it: but I found none.

Therefore have I poured out mine indignation upon them; I have consumed them with the fire of my wrath: their own way have I recompensed upon their heads, saith the Lord God.

Ezekiel 22:29-31

Another Key

Under the Old Covenant, God sought for a man to stand in the gap and make up the hedge, but He found none. Under the New Covenant, however, we have such a man: His name is *Jesus*. And we have a Comforter—the Holy Spirit. There is power on the side of the believer today. Jesus gave us His Name to use. We now have an Intercessor, who is seated at the right hand of the Father, and He makes intercession for us.

God speaks through Isaiah:

Therefore will I divide him a portion with the great, and he shall divide the spoil with the strong; because he hath poured out his soul unto death: and he was numbered with the transgressors; and he bare the sin of many, and made intercession for the transgressors.

Isaiah 53:12

Isaiah prophesied that Jesus would make intercession for the transgressors. We know that He wept over Jerusalem; He prayed for those that rejected Him. When He was on the cross He cried, "Father, forgive them; for they know not what they do" (Luke 23:34). John gives us insight on this in the light of the New Covenant:

> **My little children, these things write I unto you, that ye sin not. And if any man sin, we have an advocate with the Father, Jesus Christ the righteous:**
>
> **And he is the propitiation for our sins: and not for ours only, but also for the sins of the whole world.**
>
> **And hereby we do know that we know him, if we keep his commandments.**
>
> **1 John 2:1-3**

"If any man sin, we have an advocate with the Father." The word *advocate* in the Greek is *paraclete*. It means advocate, consoler, comforter, or intercessor.[1] The Old Testament word *intercessor* means mediator; one who intercedes; one who pleads in behalf of another. In the New Testament the word translated *intercession* means to meet with, come between; intercede. Every time the word is used referring to intercession that is done under the New Covenant, it is referring to Jesus or the Holy Spirit.

---

[1] George Ricker Berry, *Interlinear Greek-English New Testament* (Reading, Pennsylvania: Handy Book Company, copyright 1897 Hines S. Noble). Reprinted by Baker Book House, Grand Rapids, Michigan, 5th printing, 1981.

James H. Strong, *Strong's Exhaustive Concordance* (Grand Rapids: Baker Book House, 1992), "Greek Dictionary of the New Testament," p. 55, #3875.

Jesus is our *Intercessor.* He is our Counselor, our Consoler, our Comforter; in other words, our Lawyer. In making reference to the Holy Spirit as the Comforter, Jesus said, "I will not leave you comfortless: I will come to you" (John 14:18).

Jesus Christ, being our Advocate and Intercessor, pleads our case for us.

John gives us some good news: "If we confess our sins, he is faithful and just to forgive us our sins, and to cleanse us from all unrighteousness" (1 John 1:9).

The book of John was not written to sinners, *but to the Church.* All those who are born again have Jesus as their Advocate, their Comforter, and their Intercessor. But if they don't understand His present-day ministry, they may never receive the full benefits of that ministry. Only when they get a revelation of Jesus as their Intercessor will they be able to flow with His anointing and receive all the benefits of His ministry.

Adam Lost Direction

When Adam sinned, he shorted out the power charge of his human spirit, which I believe was the Holy Spirit. In Proverbs, Solomon tells us, "The spirit of man is the candle of the Lord, searching all the inward parts of the belly" (Prov. 20:27). Then the apostle Paul gives us more insight:

> For what man knoweth the things of a man, save the spirit of man which is in him? even so the things of God knoweth no man, but the Spirit of God.
>
> Now we have received, not the spirit of the world, but the spirit which is of God; that we might know the things that are freely given to us of God.
>
> 1 Corinthians 2:11,12

God uses the human spirit to enlighten us. Adam received from God by the Spirit of God through his spirit. When the power charge was disconnected, his spiritual battery went dead, and God had to deal with him on a physical rather than spiritual level.

But God has provided better things for us under the New Covenant. Paul put it this way:

> For to be carnally minded is death; but to be spiritually minded is life and peace.
>
> Because the carnal mind is enmity against God: for it is not subject to the law of God, neither indeed can be.
>
> So then they that are in the flesh cannot please God.
>
> But ye are not in the flesh, but in the Spirit, if so be that the Spirit of God dwell in you. Now if any man have not the Spirit of Christ, he is none of his.
>
> And if Christ be in you, the body is dead because of sin; but the Spirit is life because of righteousness.
>
> But if the Spirit of him that raised up Jesus from the dead dwell in you, he that raised up Christ from

the dead shall also quicken your mortal bodies by his Spirit that dwelleth in you.

Romans 8:6-11

Today the Spirit of Christ (the Holy Spirit) quickens the human spirit, brings life to the spirit man, and establishes a communication with God. God communicates with us through our spirit. "For as many as are led by the Spirit of God, they are the sons of God" (Rom. 8:14). It is God's Spirit that bears witness with our spirit that we are the sons of God.

God doesn't bear witness with our body; He bears witness with our spirit.

Even though Jesus had walked with and taught the disciples face to face, they didn't grasp much of what He taught because they were not yet born again. It makes a difference when you are born again. Jesus said to Nicodemus:

> **Verily, verily, I say unto thee, Except a man be born again, he cannot see the kingdom of God.**
>
> **That which is born of the flesh is flesh; and that which is born of the Spirit is spirit.**
>
> **Marvel not that I said unto thee, Ye must be born again.**
>
> **John 3:3,6,7**

If you are to understand or perceive the Kingdom of God, you must be born again because it is spiritually discerned.

Before Jesus left the earth, He said to His disciples:

I have yet many things to say unto you, but ye cannot bear them now.

Howbeit when he, the Spirit of truth, is come, he will guide you into all truth: for he shall not speak of himself; but whatsoever he shall hear, that shall he speak: and he will shew you things to come.

John 16:12,13

This is revelation available today under the New Covenant.

2

Intercession Under the Old Covenant

2

Intercession Under the Old Covenant

Under the Old Covenant, God dealt on a different level with His people. They did not have the Comforter or Intercessor as we have today. We can see two levels of intercession in the Bible. Under the Old Covenant, before men were born again, it was done on a natural level. But in the New Testament it was done on a supernatural level.

We see the natural level in Genesis 18 as Abraham interceded for Lot in Sodom:

> **And the Lord appeared unto him in the plains of Mamre: and he sat in the tent door in the heat of the day;**
> **And he lift up his eyes and looked, and, lo, three men stood by him: and when he saw them, he ran to meet them from the tent door, and bowed himself toward the ground.**
>
> **Genesis 18:1,2**

This was the Lord coming with two angels. Abraham had food prepared and set before them. They ate, then stood up to leave.

And the Lord said, Shall I hide from Abraham that thing which I do;

Seeing that Abraham shall surely become a great and mighty nation, and all the nations of the earth shall be blessed in him?

For I know him, that he will command his children and his household after him, and they shall keep the way of the Lord, to do justice and judgment; that the Lord may bring upon Abraham that which he hath spoken of him.

And the Lord said, Because the cry of Sodom and Gomorrah is great, and because their sin is very grievous;

I will go down now, and see whether they have done altogether according to the cry of it, which is come unto me; and if not, I will know.

And the men turned their faces from thence, and went toward Sodom: but Abraham stood yet before the Lord.

And Abraham drew near, and said, Wilt thou also destroy the righteous with the wicked?

Peradventure there be fifty righteous within the city: wilt thou also destroy and not spare the place for the fifty righteous that are therein?

That be far from thee to do after this manner, to slay the righteous with the wicked: and that the righteous should be as the wicked, that be far from thee: Shall not the Judge of all the earth do right?

Genesis 18:17-25

Notice Abraham's question is also his answer: "Shall not the judge of all the earth do right?" He was pleading his case before God, interceding on behalf of his nephew in Sodom.

> And the Lord said, If I find in Sodom fifty right-eous within the city, then I will spare all the place for their sakes.
>
> And Abraham answered and said, Behold now, I have taken upon me to speak unto the Lord, which am but dust and ashes:
>
> Peradventure there shall lack five of the fifty righteous: wilt thou destroy all the city for lack of five? And he said, If I find there forty and five, I will not destroy it.
>
> And he said, Oh let not the Lord be angry, and I will speak yet but this once: Peradventure ten shall be found there. And he said, I will not destroy it for ten's sake
>
> **Genesis 18:26-28,32**

Abraham thought he was on safe ground if God would spare the city for ten righteous. But God sent two angels to Sodom, and they did not find ten righteous, and the cities were destroyed. Yet, God would have spared them for the sake of ten righteous people.

There is something prophetic in that statement. There are many prophets of doom today who say God is going to destroy the United States of America because of the wickedness in this nation.

There is much wickedness in this nation. But we now have a man to stand in the gap and make up the hedge, One who can intercede supernaturally through Spirit-filled believers. We have millions of born-again, Spirit-filled believers who pray in the Spirit. They are channels through which Jesus can intercede supernaturally for this nation in the manner that Paul refers to in Romans 8:26-28.

There are many today who call themselves intercessors. But to be scriptural about it, Jesus is really the Intercessor. He uses the Holy Spirit to pray through them the way God would pray. No, I don't believe God will destroy the righteous with the wicked. He didn't even do that under the Old Covenant, and He has provided better things for us under the New Covenant.

Moses Intercedes for God's People

And the Lord said unto Moses, I have seen this people, and, behold, it is a stiffnecked people:

Now therefore let me alone, that my wrath may wax hot against them, and that I may consume them: and I will make of thee a great nation.

And Moses besought the Lord his God, and said, Lord, why doth thy wrath wax hot against thy people, which thou hast brought forth out of the land of Egypt with great power, and with a mighty hand?

Wherefore should the Egyptians speak, and say, For mischief did he bring them out, to slay them in the mountains, and to consume them from the face

of the earth? Turn from thy fierce wrath, and repent of this evil against thy people.

Remember Abraham, Isaac, and Israel, thy servants, to whom thou swarest by thine own self, and saidst unto them, I will multiply your seed as the stars of heaven, and all this land that I have spoken of will I give unto your seed, and they shall inherit it for ever.

And the Lord repented of the evil which he thought to do unto his people.

Exodus 32:9-14

The way the Old Testament is written, it sometimes speaks of punishment as evil, because it was certainly not good news. Moses stood between God and Israel, interceding on behalf of the children of Israel and reminding God of what He had promised.

And the Lord said unto Moses, How long will this people provoke me? and how long will it be ere they believe me, for all the signs which I have shewed among them?

I will smite them with the pestilence, and disinherit them, and will make of thee a greater nation and mightier than they.

And Moses said unto the Lord, Then the Egyptians shall hear it, (for thou broughtest up this people in thy might from among them;)

And they will tell it to the inhabitants of this land: for they have heard that thou Lord art among this people, that thou Lord art seen face to face, and that thy cloud standeth over them, and that thou goest before them, by day time in a pillar of a cloud, and in a pillar of fire by night.

Now if thou shalt kill all this people as one man, then the nations which have heard the fame of thee will speak, saying,

Because the Lord was not able to bring this people into the land which he sware unto them, therefore he hath slain them in the wilderness.

And now, I beseech thee, let the power of my Lord be great, according as thou hast spoken, saying,

The Lord is longsuffering, and of great mercy, forgiving iniquity and transgression, and by no means clearing the guilty, visiting the iniquity of the fathers upon the children unto the third and fourth generation.

Pardon, I beseech thee, the iniquity of this people according unto the greatness of thy mercy, and as thou hast forgiven this people, from Egypt even until now.

And the Lord said, I have pardoned according to thy word.

Numbers 14:11-20

Moses made what we would call intercession on a natural level, using only the knowledge he had learned from God and His Word. But he pleaded Israel's case before God and changed the course of events.

How much more can we expect to change the course of events today by allowing Jesus to intercede through us supernaturally?

But in contrast to the two covenants, let's look again at what Solomon said:

> **So I returned, and considered all the oppressions that are done under the sun: and behold the tears of such as were oppressed, and they had no comforter; and on the side of their oppressors there was power; but they had no comforter.**
>
> **Wherefore I praised the dead which are already dead more than the living which are yet alive.**
>
> **Yea, better is he than both they, which hath not yet been, who hath not seen the evil work that is done under the sun.**
>
> Ecclesiastes 4:1-3

Now that is a bad situation any way you look at it. Solomon is actually saying it would have been better not to have been born than to live in a situation where the oppressor had power, and you had no power and no comforter.

To fully understand this, we must realize that in that day the people had no Intercessor and no Comforter; neither did they have the name of Jesus. So *we should not expect to experience today what they experienced under the Old Covenant, for we have an Intercessor, a Comforter, and the New Covenant, which is established on better promises.*

Let's look again at what God had to say in the book of Ezekiel:

> **The people of the land have used oppression, and exercised robbery, and have vexed the poor and**

needy: yea, they have oppressed the stranger wrongfully.

And I sought for a man among them, that should make up the hedge, and stand in the gap before me for the land, that I should not destroy it: but I found none.

Ezekiel 22:29,30

God sought for *a man* to stand in the gap and make up the hedge, so that He would not destroy the land, but He found none.

Therefore have I poured out mine indignation upon them; I have consumed with the fire of my wrath: their own way have I recompensed upon their heads, saith the Lord God.

Ezekiel 22:31

Notice God's statement here: "...their own way have I recompensed upon their heads." In other words, what happened to them was their choice. They spoke it and it came to pass. They prophesied their own defeat. (Prov. 18:21.)

This gives us some understanding of why things happened as they did under the Old Covenant. There was no man to stand in the gap and make up the hedge that would turn away God's wrath. This is where many who prophesy doom miss it; they say God is going to destroy America because of the evil in this nation.

But we should not expect to experience under the New Covenant what they faced under the Old. Under the New

Covenant, God has a man to stand in the gap and make up the hedge: His name is Jesus! He is our Intercessor, and He makes that intercession through us here on earth.

The Body of Christ is praying the Word of God over the world, and things are being changed day by day. We've seen things happen in our day that no one expected to happen in our generation. The Berlin Wall has been brought down, communism is dead in the water, and Russia is looking toward democracy.

God's Word *is* changing the world!

3

No Justice and
No Intercessor

3

No Justice and No Intercessor

Isaiah gives us another view of what it was like in that day under the Old Covenant. Let's look again in chapter 59:

> Therefore is judgment far from us, neither doth justice overtake us: we wait for light, but behold obscurity; for brightness, but we walk in darkness.
>
> We grope for the wall like the blind, and we grope as if we had no eyes: we stumble at noon day as in the night; we are in desolate places as dead men....
>
> In transgressing and lying against the Lord, and departing away from our God, speaking oppression and revolt, conceiving and uttering from the heart words of falsehood.
>
> And judgment is turned away backward, and justice standeth afar off: for truth is fallen in the street, and equity cannot enter.
>
> Yea, truth faileth; and he that departeth from evil maketh himself a prey: and the Lord saw it, and it displeased him that there was no judgment.
>
> And he saw that there was no man, and wondered that there was no intercessor: therefore his arm

brought salvation unto him; and his righteousness, it sustained him.

For he put on righteousness as a breastplate, and an helmet of salvation upon his head; and he put on the garments of vengeance for clothing, and was clad with zeal as a cloak.

According to their deeds, accordingly he will repay, fury to his adversaries, recompense to his enemies; to the islands he will repay recompense.

So shall they fear the name of the Lord from the west, and his glory from the rising of the sun. When the enemy shall come in like a flood, the spirit of the Lord shall lift up a standard against him.

Isaiah 59:10,13-19

Do you realize you can't contain a flood? High water, yes; but a flood, no! You can use sandbags to keep the high water out for a while, but a flood cannot be contained.

This was the situation under the Old Covenant. *When the people got out from under the protection of their Covenant,* the enemy came in like a flood.

Their only umbrella of protection was the law of the Covenant. If they failed to keep it, they were legal game to the enemy. But the New Covenant is a better covenant, established on better promises, and Jesus guarantees it.

The word *flood* in verse 19 means a stream.[1] It could include a flowing stream or river; in other words, a rushing, moving torrent of water.

---

[1] James H. Strong, *Strong's Exhaustive Concordance* (Grand Rapids: Baker Book House, 1992), "Hebrew and Chaldee Dictionary," p. 77, #5104.

You can see that under the Old Covenant when the enemy came in like a flood, they were in big trouble, for they did not have an intercessor; they did not have the breastplate of righteousness or the helmet of salvation.

There is no Scripture in the Old Testament that says resist the devil and he will flee from you. Their only safety was in keeping the Law. Otherwise, the enemy could come in like a mighty, rushing torrent.

Notice the phrase, "lift up a standard." The footnote says, "put him to flight."[2] The standard was God's Word. In the book of John we find some Scriptures which I believe would relate to Isaiah 59:19 today as we are living under a better covenant:

> **In the last day, that great day of the feast, Jesus stood and cried, saying, If any man thirst, let him come unto me, and drink.**
>
> **He that believeth on me, as the scripture hath said, out of his belly shall flow rivers of living water.**
>
> **John 7:37,38**

Now let's consider Isaiah 59:19 in light of the New Testament. If you read it with the Old Covenant mentality, this would not fit; the Holy Spirit was not available to them, as He is to us today. But with our knowledge of the New Covenant, we can see that these two Scriptures are related

---

[2] *The Holy Bible: King James Version.* Kenneth Copeland Reference Edition (Fort Worth, TX: Kenneth Copeland Ministries, Inc.), p. 935. Printed in Great Britain at the University Press, Cambridge.

by the word *river* and by the phrase *rivers of flowing water.* This would be the New Testament way of looking at Isaiah 59:19: *When the enemy shall come in "like a flood," the spirit of the Lord shall lift up a standard against him.* God's Spirit flowing through your spirit lifts up that standard, which is God's Word. Notice, not just a river but *rivers.* This indicates torrents that can't be contained; in other words, a flood against the enemy.

(But this spake he of the Spirit, which they that believe on him should receive: for the Holy Ghost was not yet given; because that Jesus was not yet glorified.)

John 7:39

Again Proverbs 20:27 says, "The spirit of man is the candle of the Lord, searching all the inward parts of the belly." In this Scripture the word *belly* is referring to the innermost part of man.

Out of your innermost being (or out of your spirit, the real you) "shall flow rivers of living water." If you view Isaiah 59:19 in light of the New Testament perspective, it is God's Spirit flowing out of your spirit as a flood and a torrent that the enemy can't contain or stop, so he has no choice but to flee.

Then with the knowledge and revelation of the New Testament and its better promises, allow me to give you my own paraphrase of Isaiah 59:19, with a New Testament mentality:

When the enemy shall come in, then the Holy Spirit through your spirit shall release a river, a living torrent, of God's Word in a language of the Spirit that will flood the enemy with light and put him to flight in stark terror, with nowhere to hide.

The enemy cannot contain the Spirit of God when He begins to flow through the human spirit in supernatural tongues.

The apostle Paul gives us insight into this in the eighth chapter of Romans:

But if we hope for that we see not, then do we with patience wait for it.

Likewise the Spirit also helpeth our infirmities: for we know not what we should pray for as we ought: but the Spirit itself maketh intercession for us with groanings which cannot be uttered.

Romans 8:25,26

"The Spirit itself maketh intercession for us with groanings *which cannot be uttered."* You will notice that it was groaning in the Spirit, not the flesh; groanings which cannot be uttered in articulate speech, or in a language we have learned. We must be careful not to fall in the ditch on one side or the other, but to keep a balance. I don't believe it's scriptural to have groaning sessions.

There are times when there will be travail in the Spirit. But when it is done in the flesh, it becomes just that, a work of the flesh, which will only cause a lot of confusion.

"Groanings which cannot be uttered" means sounds that cannot be uttered in your language. When Jesus groaned, it was in the Spirit; it was a sigh of indignation. (John 11:33.) It was not a fleshly groaning. We must be careful lest we do an injustice to the Spirit of God by getting sidetracked and trying to do in the flesh what can only be done in the Spirit.

4

Supernatural Intercession

4

Supernatural Intercession

**And he that searcheth the hearts knoweth what
is the mind of the Spirit, because he maketh intercession for the saints according to *the will of* God.**

Romans 8:27

You will notice the phrase *the will of* is in italics. That
means it was not in the original text but was added by the
translators. So let's read it without that phrase: "...because
he maketh intercession for the saints *according to God.*"

Some say, "Why speak with tongues if you can't understand what is being said?"

I answer that with this question: Do you suppose it would
do any good if God prayed for you? The answer is obvious.

But prayer for people on earth must be prayed by
someone on earth, for God gave mankind dominion over it.
(Matt. 16:19; 18:19; Gen. 1:26-28.)

Since Jesus has been glorified and is seated at the
Father's right hand, He is as much God as God Himself.
That's why it is imperative that Jesus intercede, by way of

the Holy Spirit, through your spirit, using you as the earthly agent to release that prayer of intercession in the earth.

Jesus, by the Holy Spirit, uses your voice to pray the way God would pray about situations of which you have no knowledge. You can't possibly pray about or plead a case effectively before God on a natural level when you have no knowledge of that situation.

Yet, it is possible to plead your case for another on a natural level, if you have knowledge of the situation involved. Abraham interceded in his own voice. You can pray for others in your own language on a natural level. But when you intercede in the Spirit, you have connected with Jesus by way of the Holy Spirit, and He intercedes through you on a supernatural level. Then you are praying beyond your own knowledge and ability.

We Speak Mysteries

For he that speaketh in an unknown tongue speaketh not unto men, but unto God: for no man understandeth him; howbeit in the spirit he speaketh mysteries.

1 Corinthians 14:2

While praying in the Spirit, it would certainly be a mystery to you for you wouldn't know naturally (mentally) what you are praying. Paul said:

> The natural man receiveth not the things of the Spirit of God: for they are foolishness unto him: neither can he know them, because they are spiritually discerned.
>
> But he that is spiritual judgeth all things, yet he himself is judged of no man.
>
> 1 Corinthians 2:14,15

Jesus, by the Holy Spirit, discerns the situation and prays through your spirit the way God would pray.

Suppose God came to your house and you didn't have enough money to pay your bills, or the house note was due. If He said, "I'm going to pray for you," how you suppose He would pray? His prayer would probably be something like this:

"Because you have given, it is given unto you; good measure, pressed down, shaken together, and running over shall men give unto your bosom. Because you sow bountifully, you reap bountifully; and I supply all your need according to My riches in glory by Christ Jesus." (Luke 6:38; 2 Cor. 9:6; Phil. 4:19.)

God would pray His Word over your situation.

Sometimes we miss it in our praying. But when we pray in tongues, as the Holy Spirit gives utterance, we can rest assured that our Intercessor will not miss it. The Spirit of Truth has come, and He is making intercession for and through us "according to the will of God."

Then after we have prayed in that manner, we know the things we prayed about in the Spirit will begin to work together for good. Paul put it this way:

And we know that all things work together for good to them that love God, to them who are the called according to his purpose.

Romans 8:28

But we must keep this Scripture in context and in the right perspective, lest we be misled. So much of the time we hear this Scripture quoted (or should I say misquoted?) over bad things that happen, like a car wreck or a person getting sick or dying. But that was not the intent of what Paul was saying.

Let's keep this verse 28 in context. When you *pray in the Spirit* about a particular situation, the Holy Spirit through your spirit prays the way God would pray concerning that matter. Then *you know that what you prayed about in the Spirit will begin to work together for good,* because God has found *a man* to stand in the gap and make up the hedge. That Man is Christ, the Son of God, and He is our Intercessor! He knows how to release through you a living torrent of God's Word to effectively change things and to bring some good out of a bad situation.

Scripturally Legal

How is Jesus able to do that? How can He do it legally without violating the earth lease that He gave to mankind?

Even though Jesus is restored to His Godhead powers and is seated at the right hand of the Father, He is still able to make intercession for us.

> **For Christ is not entered into the holy places made with hands, which are the figures of the true; but into heaven itself, now to appear in the presence of God for us.**
>
> **Hebrews 9:24**

Today Jesus is representing us in heaven. He is there to appear in the presence of God *for us*. He represents us in heaven; and we, in effect, represent Him here on earth, as His Body. The apostle Paul said in Ephesians 2:6 that *we have been raised up together and made to sit together in heavenly places in Christ Jesus*. What a statement! But can we fathom the depth of that statement?

When He was exalted and seated at the right hand of the Father, we were raised up and made to sit *together with Him* in heavenly places. But how can we be made to sit together with Him? By being in Christ Jesus.

No, it is not through our ability but through our union with Him that we are seated with Him. We are not physically there; we are there in Christ Jesus, because our *union* with Him has made us one with Him.

Here is how Jesus put it while praying:

> **That they all may be one; as thou, Father, art in me, and I in thee, that they also may be one in us: that the world may believe that thou hast sent me.**

> **And the glory which thou gayest me I have given them; that they may be one, even as we are one:**
>
> **I in them, and thou in me, that they may be made perfect in one; and that the world may know that thou hast sent me, and hast loved them, as thou hast loved me.**
>
>

John 17:21-23

Jesus is exalted *"far above* all principality, and power, and might, and dominion, and every name that is named, not only in this world, but also in that which is to come" (Eph. 1:21). And we have been raised up together and made to sit together in heavenly places with Him!

"Christ is...entered...into heaven itself, now to appear in the presence of God for us" (Heb. 9:24). According to Hebrews 6:20 Jesus, who is the forerunner for us, has entered into heaven. He is our forerunner into heaven. He is there for our sakes, daily representing us in the presence of God.

We are here on earth representing Him, for we are His Body. We represent Him physically on earth while He represents us spiritually in heaven. If we are in Him, then as far as God is concerned, He sees us far above principalities and powers.

> **For the law having a shadow of good things to come, and not the very image of the things, can never with those sacrifices which they offered year by year continually make the comers there into perfect.**

For then would they not have ceased to be offered? because that the worshippers once purged should have had no more conscience of sins.

But in those sacrifices there is a remembrance again made of sins every year.

For it is not possible that the blood of bulls and of goats should take away sins.

Wherefore when he cometh into the world, he saith, Sacrifice and offering thou wouldest not, but a body hast thou prepared me.

Hebrews 10:1-5

You should underline verse 5 above, especially the phrase, "but a body hast thou prepared me." For Jesus to effect changes on earth today, He must have a body here to do His work. The Church is the only physical Body of Christ on earth today. Jesus came to earth in a physical flesh, blood and bone body. He was manifest in the flesh. He was the sacrificial Lamb for us. After He had accomplished His work on earth, He ascended into heaven to represent us in the presence of God.

In burnt offerings and sacrifices for sin thou hast had no pleasure.

Then said I, Lo, I come (in the volume of the book it is written of me) to do thy will, O God.

Above when he said, Sacrifice and offering and burnt offerings and offering for sin thou wouldest not, neither hadst pleasure therein; which are offered by the law;

> **Then said he, Lo, I come to do thy will, O God. He taketh away the first, that he may establish the second.**
>
> **Hebrews 10:6-9**

Jesus took away the first covenant, actually fulfilling it. When He said on the cross, "It is finished" (John 19:30), He didn't mean the plan of redemption was totally and completely finished. In essence, He was saying that the last sacrifice ever to be received by God the Father from planet Earth was finished. There would be no more sacrifice for sin.

Jesus didn't come to do away with the Law but to fulfill it, so mankind could be free from the old law of works and enter into a new and better covenant.

When you read about all the things they had to do under the Old Covenant just as an atonement for sin, you can realize we have a much better covenant. First John 1:9 is much more effective:

> **If we confess our sins, he is faithful and just to forgive us our sins, and to cleanse us from all unrighteousness.**

The New and Better Covenant needed *only one sacrifice, once for all.*

> **By the which will we are sanctified through the offering of the body of Jesus Christ once for all.**
> **And every priest standeth daily ministering and offering oftentimes the same sacrifices, which can never take away sins:**

> **But this man, after he had offered one sacrifice for sins for ever, sat down on the right hand of God;**
>
> **From henceforth expecting till his enemies be made his footstool.**
>
> **Hebrews 10:10-13**

Jesus is expecting His enemies to be put under *our* feet. In Ephesians 1:22-23 the apostle Paul says Christ is the Head of the Church and we are the Body. The feet are in the Body. Jesus is seated at the right hand of the Father until His enemies are made His footstool. He is seated there now, expecting the Body of Christ to tread Satan underfoot.

For God to come here in His divine Godhead powers and destroy the devil's work before man's lease runs out would be scripturally illegal. For He gave the earth lease to mankind and told man to have dominion over it and subdue it. (Gen. 1:26-28.)

But the Body of Christ has now been given authority on this planet through Jesus!

You have authority here because you are a legal resident; therefore you have a scriptural, legal right to destroy the works of the devil.

5

The Present-Day
Ministry of Jesus

5

The Present-Day Ministry of Jesus

Hebrews, chapter 7, refers to Melchisedec and likens him to Jesus, because the Scripture does not give any beginning or end of the lineage of Melchisedec.

> **By so much was Jesus made a surety of a better testament.**
> **And they truly were many priests, because they were not suffered to continue by reason of death:**
> **But this man, because he continueth ever, hath an unchangeable priesthood.**
> **Wherefore he is able also to save them to the uttermost that come unto God by him, seeing he ever liveth to make intercession for them.**
>
> **Hebrews 7:22-25**

Today Jesus is *alive in heaven* and *makes intercession* for us, but it helps if we know how He makes intercession.

It is illegal for God to destroy the works of the devil with His divine Godhead powers before the lease expires on this planet. (Gen. 1:26-28; 1 John 3:8.) But Jesus, by being born on this planet, had legal authority here. He healed the sick, raised the dead, and cast out demons. He destroyed the works of the devil legally until the day He died, for He was a man anointed with the Holy Ghost.

Restored to Glory

But when Jesus arose from the dead, a change had taken place. He lost His authority to operate on earth as a man. He was restored to the glory He once had before the world was in existence. He received His glorified body. He could eat with His disciples, then get up and walk through the wall. But He was no longer operating as a man. He was restored to His divine power and glory, and His ministry had changed. (John 17:5.)

It Began With the Word

Understanding the present-day ministry of Jesus and how He works in the earth today is vital in putting Satan underfoot. Jesus is *expecting* His enemies to be made His footstool. John tells us:

> **In the beginning was the Word, and the Word was with God, and the Word was God.**
> **All things were made by him; and without him was not any thing made that was made.**
> **And the Word was made flesh, and dwelt among us....**
> **John 1:1,3,14**

Jesus came in the flesh. We could say the Word took upon Itself flesh and dwelt among us. He was given a physical body—a flesh, blood and bone body. He was born of a virgin, and God was His Father. There was no sin in Him. He had the body of a man, and He could exercise authority on earth, for God had given man dominion over the earth.

God said, Let us make man in our image, after our likeness: and let them have dominion over the fish of the sea, and over the fowl of the air, and over the cattle, and over all the earth, and over every creeping thing that creepeth upon the earth.

Genesis 1:26

God gave Adam a lease on this planet, and He gave mankind dominion over it. But when Adam sinned, he turned the earth lease over to Satan. Then God had a problem on His hands. What was He going to do? He had given man a lease on the earth, but Adam had broken God's Word and sold out to the devil. The devil became, in essence, "the god of this world" (2 Cor. 4:4).

But God had a plan to get His Word back into this earth. He first made a covenant with Adam. Then He made covenants with Noah and with Moses. But the covenant He made with Abraham was the covenant of *all covenants*. It actually meant that Abraham was given access to what God had, and all Abraham had belonged to God—even his life, if God required it.

45

Abraham *knew* what that covenant meant. God's plan was to gain back some control in the earth. To do so He had to get His Son born into this earth with a physical flesh, blood, and bone body. Then Jesus would have legal authority here. Jesus had to be "in all points tempted like as we are, yet without sin" (Heb. 4:15).

When you realize what the first chapter of Genesis says, you will understand why God doesn't come back to earth and destroy the devil and all evil. To do that at the present time, God would have to violate His Word.

God is not limited in power, but He has limited Himself *by His Word!* There is a time and place for everything. He has the ability to destroy the devil and all evil, but if He were to do it now, before the lease expires, He would violate His Word. The true Church, which is the Body of Christ on earth today, has the authority to enforce Satan's defeat until we are raptured.

God has done all that *He will do* about it until the lease runs out on this planet. But when that lease expires, Satan will be put in his place. (Rev. 20:1-10.)

The Intercessory Ministry of Jesus

God is patiently waiting for the Body of Christ to *exercise our authority and dominion in putting Satan underfoot! When we understand the present-day ministry of Jesus and how He channels it through us, the Body here on earth, then we will be better equipped to enforce Satan's defeat.*

Follow closely as we look at the reasons why the effectiveness of the intercessory ministry of Jesus depends so much on the faithfulness of individual members of the Body of Christ.

Without your cooperation and that of other members of the Body of Christ, Jesus is somewhat limited in His intercessory ministry. This is a simple truth and easy to understand as we follow the Scriptures. It had been prophesied by Isaiah: "Behold, a virgin shall conceive, and bear a son, and shall call his name Immanuel" (Isa. 7:14). Jesus came into this planet legally, born of a woman. He had no earthly father; God was His Father. He had a physical body just like any other man. He walked like a man, talked like a man, got tired like a man, because He *was* a man. (Phil. 2:8; Heb. 2:16.)

Jesus was, first of all, a man; but He was also the Son of God. Yet, He called Himself the Son of Man. He had to be a man in order to have legal authority on the earth to destroy the works of the devil. Jesus gives us insight into this in John 10:1-2:

> **Verily, verily, I say unto you, He that entereth not by the door into the sheepfold, but climbeth up some other way, the same is a thief and a robber.**
> **But he that entereth in by the door is the shepherd of the sheep.**

Specifically, verse 1 is referring to Satan and verse 2 is referring to Jesus. Yet each verse includes more than that.

"He that entereth not by the door into the sheepfold, but climbeth up some other way, the same is *a thief* and *a robber.*"

Then verse 10 shows the contrast, their reason for coming to earth:

> **The thief cometh not, but for to steal, and to kill, and to destroy: I am come that they might have *life,* and that they might have it *more abundantly.***
>
> **John 10:10**

Jesus has come to give us a *more abundant life.* Satan came for three reasons: to steal, to kill, and to destroy God's creation.

"He that entereth not by the door into the sheepfold...." Satan is the one who entered illegally into the sheepfold. Here "the sheepfold" represents the earth, for Jesus said: "That which is born of the flesh is flesh; and that which is born of the Spirit is spirit" (John 3:6).

The legal entry into the earth is *being born of the flesh.* The right of entry into the Kingdom of God is *being born of the Spirit.* The fact that you have been born on this planet is important. Your birth certificate reveals the state, county, city, and date of your birth. That birth certificate is a legal document, proving you are a legal resident here on earth.

It is a legal document that proves you have authority over the devil, demons, and evil spirits. Jesus said, "He that entereth in by the door is the shepherd of the sheep." Jesus is the Shepherd; he was born on earth. "The door" simply represents legal entry into this earth. The only legal entry into this planet is to be born here. Since you were born here, you have a legal right to exercise dominion. Your physical body gives you authority here on earth.

Satan was not born here. He does not have a physical body. He is an illegal alien and has no legal authority on this planet. He gained a limited access to the earth through deception and Adam's failure to exercise dominion over him.

Satan is called "the prince of the power of the air, the spirit that now worketh in the children of disobedience" (Eph. 2:2). He is a spirit being, but he does not have a physical flesh, blood, and bone body. He has no authority to exercise dominion on earth for he was not born here. There is very little he can do unless he can get in some body.

Your birth certificate is a legal document that will stand up in the Supreme Court of this land, proving you are a legal resident of the earth. It confirms that you have legal authority here.

Jesus had to be born on earth to have legal authority here. After Adam sold the earth lease out to Satan, God couldn't come into the earth and destroy the evil works by His divine Godhead powers because He had given mankind a lease on the earth, and commanded them to exercise dominion over it.

The Earth Lease

Jesus refers to this lease by a parallel in Mark's gospel:

And he began to speak unto them by parables. A certain man planted a vineyard, and set an hedge

49

about it, and digged a place for the winefat, and built a tower, and let it out to husbandmen, and went into a far country.

And at the season he sent to the husbandmen a servant, that he might receive from the husbandmen of the fruit of the vineyard.

And they caught him, and beat him, and sent him away empty.

And again he sent unto them another servant; and at him they cast stones, and wounded him in the head, and sent him away shamefully handled.

And again he sent another; and him they killed, and many others; beating some, and killing some.

Having yet therefore one son, his wellbeloved, he sent him also last unto them, saying, They will reverence my son.

But those husbandmen said among themselves, This is the heir; come, let us kill him, and the inheritance shall be ours.

And they took him, and killed him, and cast him out of the vineyard.

Mark 12:1-8

Although this parable has dual meaning, it is no doubt a vivid description of the earth lease that was given.

To help illustrate God's situation after Adam turned the lease over to Satan, let's take a look at a natural lease.

I own a farm, which is leased out to another individual. Suppose I were to go to that farmer and say, "I don't want you to plant cotton or soybeans on my farm. I want you to plant cucumbers and tomatoes."

I know what he would say: "I have the lease so I will plant what I want to plant."

I could complain, saying, "But it's my farm!"

He would only say, "Yes, but I have a lease on it, and as long as I have that lease, I will determine what is planted on this farm."

Because he has the lease, the land is under his control. I can't do the things I want until that lease expires.

God's Dilemma

After Adam sold out the earth lease to the devil, Satan became, as Paul calls him, "the god of this world" (2 Cor. 4:4). God was in a situation where He needed a man on the earth who would walk upright, fulfilling His plan under the Old Covenant. Then it would be legal to anoint that man with the Holy Ghost and power. John tells us *why Jesus was born on this earth:*

> **...For this purpose the Son of God was manifested, that he might destroy the works of the devil.**
>
> **1 John 3:8**

And Jesus did that when He was on earth. Yet for the first thirty years of His life, He didn't heal one single person or cast out one demon.

Yes, Jesus was the Son of God! But the reason He didn't heal the sick and cast out demons before He was thirty years old was because He couldn't. He didn't have the ability. Even though He was the Son of God, He came to earth as a man. He was a legal resident here, but until God anointed Him, He did not have the ability to heal the sick or cast out demons.

Jesus walked perfect and upright under that Old Covenant for thirty years, without sin. He fulfilled the Law. When He was baptized in the River Jordan, He was anointed with the Holy Ghost and power. (Acts 10:38.)

Let's pick up on this story in Luke, chapter 4:

> **And he came to Nazareth, where he had been brought up: and, as his custom was, he went into the synagogue on the sabbath day, and stood up for to read.**
>
> **And there was delivered unto him the book of the prophet Esaias. And when he had opened the book, he found the place where it was written,**
>
> **The Spirit of the Lord is upon me, because he hath anointed me to preach the gospel to the poor; he hath sent me to heal the brokenhearted, to preach deliverance to the captives, and recovering of sight to the blind, to set at liberty them that are bruised,**
>
> **To preach the acceptable year of the Lord.**
>
> **Luke 4:16-19**

Listen to the words of Jesus: "The Spirit of the Lord is upon me, because he hath *anointed* me to preach." This is how He received the ability to heal the sick, raise the dead, cast out demons, and destroy the works of the devil: *God anointed Him.*

Jesus had authority on earth because He was born here in a physical body. But He received the ability to destroy the works of the devil when God anointed Him.

Ask yourself this question: If Jesus was God on the earth in all of His divine power, why did God have to anoint Him? Where would you go to get a higher anointing than God?

"The Spirit of the Lord is upon me, because *he hath anointed me* to preach the gospel ...to heal the broken-hearted, to preach deliverance...and recovering of sight to the blind, to set at liberty them that are bruised." God *anointed Him* with the Holy Ghost and power. It was not something that was inherent in Him as being the Son of God.

It was legal for Jesus to destroy the works of the devil because He was a legal resident of the earth. He had walked perfect and upright under the Old Covenant, which no other man had been able to do. Yes, Jesus was the Son of God; but, first of all, He was a man. He was not operating in His divine power and glory as God when He destroyed the works of the devil. He was drawing from the anointing God had placed upon Him as a man.

Humanity of Jesus

Sometimes people misunderstand what is being said when you refer to the humanity of Jesus. They think you are denying His deity or denying He was the Son of God. But that is not true. Certainly Jesus was divine and He was the Son of God, yet He was a man!

Let's look at some Scriptures that help us to understand the humanity of Jesus:

> **Let this mind be in you, which was also in Christ Jesus:**
>
> **Who, being in the form of God, thought it not robbery to be equal with God:**
>
> **But made himself of no reputation, and took upon him the form of a servant, and was made in the likeness of men:**
>
> **And being found in fashion as a man, he humbled himself, and became obedient unto death, even the death of the cross.**
>
> **Wherefore God also hath highly exalted him, and given him a name which is above every name.**
>
> **Philippians 2:5-9**

Jesus stripped Himself of this divine power and glory when He came to this earth.

> **Forasmuch then as the children are partakers of flesh and blood, he also himself likewise took part of the same; that through death he might destroy him that had the power of death, that is, the devil;**
>
> **And deliver them who through fear of death were all their lifetime subject to bondage.**
>
> **For verily he took not on him the nature of angels; but he took on him the seed of Abraham.**

Wherefore in all things it behoved him to be made like unto his brethren, that he might be a merciful and faithful high priest in things pertaining to God, to make reconciliation for the sins of the people.

For in that he himself hath suffered being tempted, he is able to succour them that are tempted.

Hebrews 2:14-18

Here we see the humanity of Jesus. He took upon Himself the seed of Abraham, being made like unto His brother. He suffered being tempted so that He would be able to help those who are tempted.

For we have not an high priest which cannot be touched with the feeling of our infirmities; but was in all points tempted like as we are, yet without sin.

Hebrews 4:15

Here we have positive proof that Jesus suffered temptation. It says He was "in all points tempted like as we are, yet without sin." Then James gives us positive proof that Jesus was not here on earth as God but as a man:

Blessed is the man that endureth temptation: for when he is tried, he shall receive the crown of life, which the Lord hath promised to them that love him.

Let no man say when he is tempted, I am tempted of God: for *God cannot be tempted with evil,* neither tempteth he any man.

James 1:12,13

These Scriptures give us great insight and positive proof into the humanity of Jesus, for God cannot be tempted with evil. Jesus was tempted in every way like we are, but He was without sin. So if Jesus had been operating as God here on earth, then it would have been impossible for Him to be tempted.

> **Though he were a Son, yet learned he obedience by the things which he suffered;**
>
> **And being made perfect, he became the author of eternal salvation unto all them that obey him.**
>
> **Hebrews 5:8,9**

Jesus learned to overcome temptation as a man, even while He was the Son of God.

Jesus Gives More Proof

> **And now, O Father, glorify thou me with thine own self with the glory which I had with thee before the world was.**
>
> **John 17:5**

In this prayer from John's gospel, Jesus asked His Father God to restore Him to the glory He once had before He was born on earth. From these Scriptures it is clear that while here on earth Jesus did not operate in His divine power and glory but as a man anointed with the Holy Ghost and power.

Jesus was perfectly legal because He was born here; He came through the legal entry into the earth, being born of a woman. But Satan has no legal authority here; he was not born on this earth. Neither were demons and evil spirits; they are illegal aliens to this planet!

If the devil comes around your house or business causing trouble, if you don't know anything else to do, *get out your birth certificate* and read it to him. Then ask him for his; he doesn't have one. When he finds out you know he doesn't have any legal authority on earth, he won't stay around long.

Satan has no legal authority on this planet. He pulled a con job on Adam and Eve, and he is still trying the same thing today.

In Ephesians 4:27 the apostle Paul says, "Give no place to the devil." Satan has no authority here unless you allow him to use yours. His only hope is in trying to usurp *your authority!*

James 4:7 says, "Submit yourselves therefore to God. *Resist the devil, and he will flee from you.*"

6

Jesus' Ministry
Depends on You

6

Jesus' Ministry Depends on You

One day as Jesus was passing the pool of Bethesda He saw a man who had been crippled for thirty-eight years. He said to that man, "Rise, take up thy bed, and walk." The man took up his bed and went home, but he was the only one in that multitude who was healed that day. (John 5:1-8.)

You would think that after Jesus arose from the dead in His glorified body, surely He would go back to the pool of Bethesda and heal that whole multitude of sick people. Surely He would go to the hospital and heal all the people who were sick. But *He didn't.*

In fact, as astounding as it may seem, after He arose from the dead, He didn't heal *one single person* by ministering personally to people. He didn't do one single miracle.

Now don't misunderstand me; Jesus is still healing people today, but not by personally laying hands on them or physically touching them as He did before He died. Today He does it through people who will allow the same anointing that was upon Him to flow through them in manifestation of the Holy Spirit and through the prayer of faith. Before He ascended to the Father, He said, "All power is given unto me in heaven and in earth" (Matt. 28:18).

In Mark 16 Jesus, in essence, said to believers, "Now *you* go *in My Name,* and *you* cast out demons; *you* speak with new tongues; *you* lay hands on the sick and they shall recover." (Mark 16:15-18.)

Jesus couldn't do it anymore because He had been glorified, so He is saying to us, "Now, it's up to *you* to destroy the works of the devil"—He turned the earthly authority and heavenly anointing over to believers. He gave us the power of attorney to use His Name.

Remember, Jesus said, "As long as I am in the world, I am the light of the world" (John 9:5). And then referring to the Body of Christ, He said, "Ye are the light of the world" (Matt. 5:14).

There was a change in Jesus' ministry after He arose from the dead and received His glorified body. Now He is as much God as God is God in all of His divine power and glory.

But He didn't heal any that were sick, or cast out any demons, or do any miracles on this earth from the time that He arose from the dead till He ascended to heaven. He had lost His authority to operate as a man. Once He had been restored to His divine power and glory, it was illegal for Him to do so.

For God said, "Let us make man in our image...and let them have dominion" (Gen. 1:26). Notice He didn't say, "Let

God in all His divine power subdue the earth and have dominion over it." He said, "Let *them* have dominion."

When Jesus arose from the dead and was restored to His divine power and glory, He gave up His right to operate as a man on the earth. So it was necessary for Him to delegate that responsibility to those on earth who had a physical flesh, blood, and bone body.

Yes, God is still God, and He has prophesied from the beginning what the end results will be. But today God uses you, the believer, as His agent to carry out His work. God furnishes the anointing, but your body gives *you the authority on earth to destroy the works of the devil.*

> **For as the Father hath life in himself; so hath he given to the Son to have life in himself;**
>
> **And hath given him authority to execute judgment also, *because he is the Son of man.***
>
> **John 5:26,27**

As a man anointed of the Holy Ghost, Jesus destroyed the works of the devil. Certainly He was the Son of God. But He had authority to do it because He was the Son of Man!

We also were born on the earth, and we have *legal authority here to destroy the works of the devil.* The present-day ministry of Jesus seems to be limited to what He can get the Body of Christ to do in His Name and by allowing His intercession to flow through that Body.

All the things that Jesus did in His earth walk were done under the Old Covenant. And we have a better covenant, established on better promises. (Heb. 8:6.) Jesus is the Guarantee of this New Covenant.

Under the Old Covenant, the blood of bulls and goats only covered sin; it could not take away the consciousness of sin. But under the New Covenant, *the blood of Jesus removes the very consciousness of sin.* Because of 1 John 1:9, we as believers have an Advocate with the Father, Jesus Christ, the Righteous. (1 John 2:1.)

Under the Old Covenant, the people didn't have an intercessor. God searched for a man who would stand in the gap and make up the hedge for Israel, but He found no one.

But now God has *a man!* We now have a High Priest who ever lives and makes intercession for us: His name is Jesus! First John 1:9 was written to the Church:

If we confess our sins, he is faithful and just to forgive us our sins, and to cleanse us from all unrighteousness.

When we make a mistake, we don't *run from* God; we *run to* God. Jesus is our representative before God in heaven. The blood of Jesus removes the very consciousness of sin. If we walk in fellowship with Him, we should have *no sin consciousness* under this New Covenant.

Here is how the apostle Paul put it:

And you, that were sometime alienated and enemies in your mind by wicked works, yet now hath he reconciled

In the body of his flesh through death, to present you holy and unblameable and unreproveable in his sight.

Colossians 1:21,22

The blood of Jesus and 1 John 1:9 give us the privilege to walk upright under this New Covenant as though sin had never existed, and God can legally anoint us with Holy Ghost power to destroy the works of the devil.

In the Scriptures we see a great change in Peter's life after the day of Pentecost. Before he had gone to the upper room, it seems that he couldn't do anything right. He went fishing and fished on the wrong side of the boat! He ran a race to the tomb and lost it!

But *he came out of that upper room anointed with the Holy Ghost*. To the first crippled man he saw, he said: "Silver and gold have I none; but such as I have give I thee: In the name of Jesus Christ of Nazareth rise up and walk.... And he leaping up stood, and walked, and entered with them into the temple, walking, and leaping, and praising God" (Acts 3:6,8).

What had happened to Peter? He became a different man after the "Acts 2:4 experience." It was very evident that what Jesus had said concerning the Holy Ghost was now being manifest in Peter's life. Notice what Jesus said to His disciples concerning the Holy Ghost:

But ye shall receive power, after that the Holy Ghost is come upon you: and ye shall be witnesses

unto me both in Jerusalem, and in all Judaea, and in
Samaria, and unto the uttermost part of the earth.

Acts 1:8

The present-day ministry of Jesus is linked to the Holy
Spirit within you.

Verily, verily, I say unto you, He that believeth
on me, the works that I do shall he do also; and
greater works than these shall he do; because I go
unto my Father.

John 14:12

These things have I spoken unto you, being yet
present with you.

But the Comforter, which is the Holy Ghost,
whom the Father will send in my name, he shall
teach you all things, and bring all things to your
remembrance, whatsoever I have said unto you.

John 14:25,26

Notice the phrase, "the Holy Ghost, whom the Father
will send in my name." Here we get some insight into the
Holy Spirit. The Comforter is "the Holy Ghost, whom the
Father will send in my name." He is called the Spirit of
Christ. (Rom. 8:9; 1 Pet. 1:11.) As Jesus said, the Holy Ghost
would be sent by the Father "in my name" and "he shall
teach you all things."

But when the Comforter is come, whom I will
send unto you from the Father, even the Spirit of

truth, which proceedeth from the Father, he shall testify of me:

And ye also shall bear witness, because ye have been with me from the beginning.

John 15:26,27

Then in John 16:7 Jesus says:

I tell you the truth; It is expedient for you that I go away: for if I go not away, the Comforter will not come unto you; but if I depart, I will send him unto you.

In other words, He was saying, "You will be better off after I am gone."

In Luke 12:50 Jesus said, "I have a baptism to be baptized with; and how am I straitened till it be accomplished!" For Jesus could only be in one place at a time. He was limited to a physical human body until death released Him.

Even though Jesus is bodily seated at the right hand of the Father, He has come back to us in the Person of the Holy Spirit to dwell in us.

I have yet many things to say unto you, but ye cannot bear them now.

Howbeit when he, the Spirit of truth, is come, he will guide you into all truth: for he shall not speak of himself; but whatsoever he shall hear, that shall he speak: and he will shew you things to come.

John 16:12,13

Allow me to paraphrase these verses: "When I come back to you in the Person of the Holy Spirit, I am going to reveal things to you that you can't comprehend without the revelation of the Holy Ghost."

And Jesus is doing that today. He is revealing these things by His Spirit to our human spirits. It is the Spirit of Truth who guides us into all truth and shows us things to come. (1 Cor. 2:9-16.)

7

Intercession Through Your Spirit

7

Intercession Through Your Spirit

But if we hope for that we see not, then do we with patience wait for it.

Likewise the Spirit also helpeth our infirmities: for we know not what we should pray for as we ought: but the Spirit itself maketh intercession for us with groanings which cannot be uttered.

And he that searcheth the hearts knoweth what is the mind of the Spirit, because he maketh intercession for the saints according to the will of God.

And we know that all things work together for good to them that love God, to them who are the called according to his purpose.

Romans 8:25-28

What is Paul referring to here when he says "all things work together for good"? We know he is *not* saying that everything that happens to us in life works together for good. He is referring to all things that Jesus, our Intercessor, prayed through our spirits by the Holy Spirit. Look again at verse 27. He that searches the heart and He that makes intercession is Christ. This is made plain in verse 34:

71

Who is he that condemneth? It is Christ that died, yea rather, that is risen again, who is even at the right hand of God, who also maketh intercession for us.

Jesus Christ today is able to join together with our spirits and pray the way God would pray. And God's way of praying will turn bad circumstances into good. This is the result of what is called *praying in the Spirit*.

In 1 Corinthians 14:14-15 Paul said:

For if I pray in an unknown tongue, my spirit prayeth, but my understanding is unfruitful.

What is it then? I will pray with the spirit, and I will pray with the understanding also....

There have been times in my life when in the natural I didn't know *how* to pray or what to pray for. But as I prayed in the Spirit, out of my spirit would come revelation. The Spirit of Truth gave me insight into things I needed to know.

Word of Knowledge by the Spirit

Several years ago I was involved in putting together a business deal. While I was sitting in the banker's office, he said to me, "We can't loan that amount of money on that farm because the second mortgage is too large."

As I was sitting there praying in the Spirit under my breath, I heard these words coming up in my spirit: *Go across the street to the other bank.*

I thought, *That's ridiculous! I've never done any business with that bank!*

As I kept praying in the Spirit, it came to me again: *Go across the street to the other bank.* So I did what I heard in my spirit.

When I told the other bank president what I needed, he said, "I heard about the farm you bought. Bring the papers; we'll loan you the whole amount if you want it."

That revelation came by the Spirit of God. This is part of the present-day ministry of Jesus: showing us things to come. Sometimes He does it through a word of knowledge or word of wisdom.

Have you ever been in a situation where you didn't know what to do? Maybe things around you were happening so fast that you didn't know how to pray and didn't have time to pray. But somehow everything turned out all right. Then a few days later you got a letter from someone saying, "I was impressed by the Spirit of God to pray for you a few days ago." The time of day that person was led to pray for you was the exact time you were in great need of supernatural help. That has happened to me several times.

Revealed by the Spirit

Several years ago I was flying a Cessna 310 on my way home from a meeting in St. Louis, Missouri. It was winter time, and I was on an instrument flight in the clouds. I flew into some freezing rain, and that can be bad news quick! Ice can build up on an airplane as fast as an inch a minute, and in just a few minutes you can get more ice than you can carry. The windshield froze over, and I could hear ice coming off the props and hitting the fuselage of the plane.

I had asked the air traffic controller for permission to change altitudes. But he was too busy to talk to me. Right at that moment I thought I was the only one on earth that knew I was in trouble.

I found out later that a man who lived 800 miles away had been impressed to pray for me in the Spirit. He didn't know what I needed, but Jesus, our Intercessor, did. By being sensitive to the Holy Spirit, that man allowed Jesus to make intercession for me through him that day.

A few days later his wife wrote me a letter and asked what had happened to me on that day, about 2:00 in the afternoon. She said her husband was led by the Spirit of God to pray in tongues; he knew it was for me but really didn't know what he was praying about. That man didn't know what my problem was or how to pray about my situation in the natural. Yet Jesus, through the Spirit of Truth in that man, made intercession for me. What he prayed about in the Spirit worked for my good.

Once I was able to get through to the air traffic controller, he gave me a different altitude, and I was out of that freezing rain within minutes.

Then a few months later another lady wrote and said, "I was impressed to pray for you in tongues on a certain day, and I had no idea why, but I prayed until I got a release in the Spirit."

When I looked at my calendar, I saw on that day we were in an airport in Little Rock, waiting for our flight. The airport had just closed down because of fog and freezing rain. At first they had said there would be no airplanes coming in that day, but later they said, "An American Airlines flight (which was our flight) is going to make an approach to see if he can see the runway. But if he can't, that is the last flight for the day."

They made the approach, broke through the fog, and landed. We were able to make it to our destination on time. Later we found out that was the *only* airplane able to land there all day!

Jesus interceded by the Holy Spirit through someone who didn't even know what the circumstance was, much less how to pray. The Holy Spirit prayed through her spirit the way God would pray, and it was legal, for she was a legal resident of this earth. If she had not responded, things could have been very different.

This is the ministry of Jesus, our Intercessor. But if He cannot get some believers to yield to the Holy Spirit, He is somewhat limited in what He can do. For the Body of Christ is the Body Jesus has on earth today that He can work through.

The physical body of Jesus gave Him the authority to destroy the works of the devil when He was on earth. Now Jesus is glorified, seated at the Father's right hand. He is

the Head and we are the Body. But now He makes intercession through us, for our physical body gives Him authority
to do so.

If Jesus is to pray for us today, He must do it through
some *body* on earth. You notice in the Scriptures that Jesus
didn't heal any sick or cast out any demons from the time
that He arose from the dead until He ascended into heaven.
He is still in the healing business, but He does it through
believers anointed by the Holy Spirit or by the prayer of
faith. (Matt. 28:18-20; Mark 16:15-20; James 5:14,15.)

Ask yourself this question: Is it legal for Jesus to pray for
us in heaven after being restored to His divine power and
glory? He is as much God as God is God or the Holy Spirit is
God. If God were to pray for you, who would He pray to?
From what I see in the Scriptures, I believe it is scripturally
illegal for God to pray in heaven for us on earth. He gave the
earth lease to mankind and told them to subdue it and have
dominion over it. (Ps. 115:16; Gen. 1:26-28; Ps. 8:3-6.)

This is why the present-day ministry of Jesus as our
Intercessor is linked to the Body of Christ here on earth. If
the Body of Christ will not respond to the unction of the Holy
Spirit to pray in the Spirit for those who are in desperate
need of supernatural help, then He is severely limited in His
intercessory ministry.

But Jesus has a scriptural right to pray supernaturally,
through the Holy Spirit in you here on earth. For you have a
body and you are a member of the Body of Christ. That gives
you authority here on earth today.

Paul said when we don't know how to pray as we ought, the Holy Spirit helps our infirmities or our inability to comprehend how and what to pray for.

I believe there have been many tragedies which would never have happened *if* the Body of Christ had been more sensitive to the intercessory ministry of Jesus, allowing Him to make intercession through their spirits here on earth.

Since He is seated at the right hand of the Father, He has to do it through someone on earth. We as believers are the Body of Christ on earth today, to which Jesus has delegated authority.

> **And Jesus came and spake unto them, saying, All power is given unto me in heaven and in earth.**
>
> **Go ye therefore...**
>
> **Matthew 28:18,19**

Mark records it this way:

> **And he said unto them, Go ye into all the world, and preach the gospel to every creature.**
>
> **He that believeth and is baptized shall be saved; but he that believeth not shall be damned.**
>
> **And these signs shall follow them that believe; In my name shall they cast out devils; they shall speak with new tongues;**
>
> **They shall take up serpents; and if they drink any deadly thing, it shall not hurt them; they shall lay hands on the sick, and they shall recover.**

So then after the Lord had spoken unto them, he was received up into heaven, and sat on the right hand of God.

And they went forth, and preached every where, the Lord working with them, and confirming the word with signs following. Amen.

Mark 16:15-20

Mark 16:15-20 is a confirmation of that authority being exercised by believers.

Then in 1 Corinthians 12:27 Paul said, "Now ye are the body of Christ, and members in particular." You are the Body that Christ must use on earth, for you have God-given authority on earth.

In Matthew 18:19 Jesus said, "...if two of you shall agree on earth...." The agreement or prayer must be on earth. It seems that He has to do it through a legal resident here. You are of that Body that can be used to stop the works of the devil on earth. Heavenly intervention is available to us, but that request must come through someone here on earth.

Therefore, it was legal for God to anoint Jesus with the Holy Ghost and healing power because Jesus was born here, and that body gave Him authority on earth. Jesus was the Son of God, yet He was a man. It was after He was baptized in the River Jordan that the anointing of God came upon Him, and it was for the purpose of destroying the works of the devil.

Let's look again in Luke, the fourth chapter, where Jesus stood up in the synagogue and read from the prophet Isaiah, concerning Himself:

> **The Spirit of the Lord is upon me, because he hath anointed me to preach the gospel to the poor; he hath sent me to heal the brokenhearted, to preach deliverance to the captives, and recovering of sight to the blind, to set at liberty them that are bruised,**
>
> **To preach the acceptable year of the Lord.**
>
> **Luke 4:18,19**

Jesus was a legal resident with earthly authority, but God's anointing gave Him the ability to destroy the works of the devil.

The first sermon Jesus preached was in the synagogue in His hometown, and the religious people tried to kill Him. He passed through their midst and went to Capernaum. (Luke 4:28-31.)

> **And in the synagogue there was a man, which had a spirit of an unclean devil, and cried out with a loud voice,**
>
> **Saying, Let us alone; what have we to do with thee, thou Jesus of Nazareth? art thou come to destroy us? I know thee who thou art; the Holy One of God.**
>
> **Luke 4:33,34**

Here we see that a demon was challenging the authority of Jesus. You would have thought the demon would have said, "He's a false prophet! Don't believe Him!" But here was a demon, witnessing for Jesus.

Why in the world would a demon witness for Jesus, saying He was "the Holy One of God"? In his own words, the demon was actually saying to Jesus: "I know who You are, and it's illegal for You to cast me out, because You're God. You gave dominion of this earth to man, so You can't cast me out. *It's illegal,* for the Scriptures say it is impossible for God to lie. You will have to violate Your Word if You cast me out."

Allow me to paraphrase what Jesus said: "Shut your mouth and come out of him!" The demon was confused, but he obeyed the command of Jesus.

Matthew gives us another account of the demons challenging the authority of Jesus to cast them out before time:

> **And when he was come to the other side into the country of the Gergesenes, there met him two possessed with devils, coming out of the tombs, exceeding fierce, so that no man might pass by that way.**
>
> **And, behold, they cried out, saying, What have we to do with thee, Jesus, thou Son of God? art thou come hither to torment us before the time?**
>
> **Matthew 8:28,29**

It's evident here in this passage of Scripture that the demons were challenging the authority of Jesus to cast them out for it wasn't time yet. What time were they referring to?

The time when the lease on this earth expires. (Rev. 10:1-7; 11:15; 20:2.)

They knew there was a time set, and they knew that God could not change that time. It's already set. But they didn't realize that Jesus was not operating as God; He was operating as a man, anointed with the Holy Ghost. It was perfectly legal for Him to destroy the works of the devil at any time by the anointing of God.

Satan could not handle *one man* operating totally in the Spirit. Jesus, walking perfect and upright under that Old Covenant, was more than Satan could handle. Every time he would come against Jesus in the way of temptation, Jesus would say, "It is written...," quoting only what God said in His Word.

Those three words shook Satan's kingdom beyond repair: *"It is written,* That man shall not live by bread alone, but by every word of God" (Luke 4:4). Satan knew what Jesus came to do, so he attempted to get Him sidetracked. By quoting Scripture out of context, he tried to deceive Jesus into jumping off the temple to His death. Satan's purpose was to destroy Jesus' physical body, for He was to be the final sacrifice. But Satan couldn't stand against the Word of God that Jesus spoke, so he departed from Him for a season.

In Hebrews 10:5 we find these words of revelation concerning Jesus being the last sacrifice under the Old Covenant: "Sacrifice and offering thou wouldest not, but a body hast thou prepared me."

Jesus put away sin by the sacrifice of Himself. We have a sinner problem, but we don't have a sin problem. Jesus was *the cure* for our sin problem.

The physical body of Jesus gave Him authority to operate on this earth. It gave Him authority to execute judgment and justice for us and against the devil.

> **For as the Father hath life in himself; so hath he given to the Son to have life in himself;**
>
> **And hath given him authority to execute judgment also, because he is the *Son of man.***
>
> **John 5:26,27**

As Acts 10:38 tells us, "God anointed Jesus of Nazareth with the Holy Ghost and with power: who went about doing good, and healing all that were oppressed of the devil; for God was with him."

Jesus had the authority to do it as a man, but He did not have the ability to destroy the works of the devil *until* God anointed Him.

It is also important for you to understand the authority your physical body gives you! I am convinced this is the key to the Body of Christ operating in its full potential as God intended.

> **Let this mind be in you, which was also in Christ Jesus:**
>
> **Who, being in the form of God, thought it not robbery to be equal with God:**

But made himself of no reputation....

Philippians 2:5-7

In other words, He thought it was not a thing to be grasped or held on to. He actually stripped Himself of His divine power and glory when He came to the earth.

...and took upon him the form of a servant, and was made in the likeness of men:

And being found in fashion as a man, he humbled himself, and became obedient unto death, even the death of the cross.

Wherefore God also hath highly exalted him, and given him a name which is above every name:

That at the name of Jesus every knee should bow, of things in heaven, and things in earth, and things under the earth.

Philippians 2:7-10

Let's say *beings,* for *things* don't have knees. At the name of Jesus every knee should bow, of *beings* in heaven, *beings* in earth, *beings* under the earth.

"And that every tongue should confess that Jesus Christ is Lord, to the glory of God the Father" (v. 11).

For years I thought this Scripture said every knee would bow to Jesus, but it says every knee shall bow *to the name of Jesus.*

We have authority in heaven, in earth, and under the earth. The name of Jesus gives us authority in three worlds.

Jesus was fashioned as a man, and this is vital to understanding our authority on the earth.

For years I thought that God and the devil were almost the same in power, and that the reason it was taking so long to get it settled about good and evil was because they were still fighting to see who would win!

Then I read the back of The Book (Revelation) and found out Jesus has already won the battle. The end is already established. The devil is defeated. God is exalted. We are more than conquerors through Jesus, our Intercessor. But He is waiting patiently for the earth lease to expire.

8

Our Right To
Exercise Dominion

8

Our Right To Exercise Dominion

The first chapter of Genesis gives us an understanding of the authority God gave to man. Then as we study other Scriptures, from the Old Testament and into the New Testament, we find this thread of truth throughout the Bible: that God uses mankind as His agents here on earth to do His work.

God made Adam, under Him, the ruler of this world. But Adam sinned and turned his authority of the earth lease over to Satan. Then Satan became what the apostle Paul called "the god of this world" (2 Cor. 4:4).

Immediately God began to make covenants with men. First He made a covenant with Adam, then He made covenants with Moses, Noah, and Abraham.

There were certain things God could not do in this earth unless He had made a covenant with a man who had legal authority here, for God had given mankind authority to rule on earth. This is a bone of contention with many religious people. Yet the Scriptures are quite clear on this matter.

Someone wrote me some time ago and said, "I don't believe God had to have access into the earth through a covenant agreement with man. If that is true, how did God destroy the world with a flood?" The answer is that God made a covenant with Noah. (Gen. 6:18; 7:1.)

There were some things God could do. But He limited Himself concerning what He could do in the earth by His Word, and God will not violate His Word. Therefore, He made covenants with men on earth so He could work through those covenants to change things on earth.

When we understand God's Word concerning how we fit into His plan, we find that we are not just strangers and pilgrims struggling through this life. But we are sons of God, created in the image and likeness of God. We have a God-given right to exercise dominion on this earth under God's covenant with man. (Gen. 17:9,10; 1 John 3:2.)

Remember Jesus' statement, "...a body hast thou prepared me" (Heb. 10:5). Jesus had been given a body. He was the sacrificial Lamb. His physical body was also His badge of authority to exercise dominion on this planet.

Even though He had authority before He was thirty years old, He didn't exercise dominion over the works of the devil until the Holy Ghost came upon Him. Every person who is born on this earth has a certain amount of legal authority, but they don't have supernatural ability to destroy the works of the devil until they are anointed with the Holy Ghost and power.

The same Holy Ghost anointing that was upon Jesus of Nazareth is available to His Body today. Before Jesus ascended to heaven, He commanded His disciples to not leave Jerusalem "until ye be endued with power from on high" (Luke 24:49). They already had authority, but they did not have ability except as Jesus had delegated to them the right to use His credit card for healing, so to speak. For Jesus had not yet died; the stripes were not yet on His back. But Jesus gave them authority to use His MasterCard and sign His Name.

And when he had called unto him his twelve disciples, he gave them power against unclean spirits, to cast them out, and to heal all manner of sickness and all manner of disease.

Matthew 10:1

And into whatsoever city ye enter, and they receive you, eat such things as are set before you:

And heal the sick that are therein, and say unto them, The kingdom of God is come nigh unto you.

Luke 10:8,9

Jesus gave them the power of attorney to use His Name to sign His MasterCard and put healing on His account until He suffered the stripes and wounds for our healing.

It is possible to have authority but no power, or you can have power but no authority.

89

For instance, when someone robs a bank, he has a weapon (power), but he has no authority to be there. If there is a policeman in the bank who has been disarmed, he has no power, but he does have authority. Yet he is limited in his ability to exercise that authority if he doesn't have the power to do so.

A policeman, because of his authority, can stop an eighteen-wheeler on the highway by holding up his hand. Although he can't physically stop the force of that truck, with his body he can exercise the authority of his commission.

By the same token, Jesus has access into the earth today through His Body, the Church. "...a body hast thou prepared me." This is referring not only to His personal body, which is in heaven, but to His spiritual Body (the Church), which is the only physical representative of Jesus Christ on earth today.

Paul said, *"Ye are the body of Christ,* and members in particular" (1 Cor. 12:27). What could Jesus do on earth today without a body? He is seated at the right hand of the Father until His enemies are made His footstool. (Matt. 22:44.)

What can He personally do about the situation here on earth? Here are His own words:

> **I will pray the Father, and he shall give you another Comforter, that he may abide with you for ever;**
>
> **Even the Spirit of truth; whom the world cannot receive, because it seeth him not, neither knoweth**

him: but ye know him; for he dwelleth with you, and shall be in you.

I will not leave you comfortless: I will come to you.

John 14:16-18

He said He would come to us, and He has come, in the Person of the Holy Spirit, to live in every believer. He is seated at the right hand of the Father in His glorified body, yet He lives inside us today.

"...a body hast thou prepared me." This simple phrase reveals such profound truth, for the only body Jesus has on this planet today is made up of believers. The Church is called the Body of Christ. *He is now depending on this Body for His authority on the earth.*

Without the Body of Christ on earth, Jesus, our Intercessor, would be severely limited in His ability to change things on earth until the lease expires. When He was physically here, His bodily presence gave Him authority. But now the Church, as the Body of Christ, has become His legal agent and authority on earth, which gives Him the legal right to furnish the ability (anointing) to destroy the works of the devil.

Concerning Principalities and Powers

Finally, my brethren, be strong in the Lord, and in the power of his might.

Put on the whole armour of God, that ye may be able to stand against the wiles of the devil.

> **For we wrestle not against flesh and blood, but against principalities, against powers, against the rulers of the darkness of this world, against spiritual wickedness in high places.**
>
> **Ephesians 6:10-12**

Paul admonishes us, "Be strong in the Lord, and in the power of his might." Notice that he does not say a thing about us being strong in ourselves. But we are His Body here on earth and joint-heirs with Him! We ought to be strong in the Lord and in the power of His might. If we have put on "the whole armour of God," we will be able to stand. And we ought to be smart enough not to take the armor off!

Paul says we wrestle not against flesh and blood. One of the problems we all face at one time or another is meeting an individual who is seemingly inspired of the devil to harass us in some way. If we are not walking in the Spirit, we will get into strife with that individual. And James says, "Where envying and strife is, there is confusion and every evil work" (James 3:16).

So we must not wrestle against flesh and blood, but we must take authority over the spirit that is driving that person.

In Daniel, chapter 10, we find a prime example of the rulers of darkness hindering the answer to Daniel's prayers. Daniel was fasting and praying concerning his vision. He says:

> **In those days I Daniel was mourning three full weeks.**

I ate no pleasant bread, neither came flesh nor wine in my mouth, neither did I anoint myself at all, till three whole weeks were fulfilled.

And in the four and twentieth day of the first month, as I was by the side of the great river, which is Hiddekel;

Then I lifted up mine eyes, and looked, and behold a certain man clothed in linen, whose loins were girded with fine gold of Uphaz:

Then said he unto me, Fear not, Daniel: for from the first day that thou didst set thine heart to understand, and to chasten thyself before thy God, thy words were heard, and I am come for thy words.

Daniel 10:2-5,12

Why did the angel come to Daniel? Because of Daniel's words. In my study of angels I have found that angels get involved in the affairs of people because of their words; either *their* prayers or *their* words. James said, "Is any among you afflicted? let him pray" (James 5:13).

In Acts 10:4 an angel came to Cornelius's house and said to him, "Thy prayers and thine alms are come up for a memorial before God." Mankind has the right and authority to pray and receive supernatural intervention from heaven on their behalf.

Daniel had been in mourning three weeks, and the angel said:

...for from the first day that thou didst set thine heart to understand, and to chasten thyself before

93

WHEN JESUS PRAYS THROUGH YOU

**thy God, thy words were heard, and I am come for
thy words.**

**But the prince of the kingdom of Persia with-
stood me one and twenty days: but, lo, Michael, one
of the chief princes, came to help me; and I remained
there with the kings of Persia.**

**Now I am come to make thee understand what
shall befall thy people in the latter days: for yet the
vision is for many days.**

Daniel 10:12-14

The angel had to battle his way through the principalities and powers. It wasn't that God didn't want Daniel's
prayers to be answered. But there were alien spirits on this
planet that had set up a kingdom in the atmosphere above
the earth, trying to stop heavenly intervention from coming
down to earth. So it took time for the angels to break through
that kingdom of darkness to bring the answer.

This is why it is so vital for you to understand the
authority you have as a legal resident of this earth, to exercise your God-given authority over principalities, powers,
and rulers of darkness concerning your situation in life.

God has highly exalted Jesus and given Him a Name
which is above every name, that at the Name of Jesus every
knee should bow—of beings in heaven, beings in earth, and
beings under the earth.

We are the Body of Christ on earth, and Jesus has given
us His Name to use in exercising dominion and putting it on
His account—the true MasterCard.

9

God Has Control
of End Results

9

God Has Control of End Results

Someone has stated, "It seems God will do nothing in the earth unless someone on earth prays for it, decrees it, or requests it."

Sometimes this question comes up: "Why doesn't God destroy all wickedness and straighten everything out here on earth?" He can't do that until the lease runs out, for He gave man a lease on the earth and commanded him to have dominion over it.

Maybe you have seen this bumper sticker: *God has everything under control.* As someone has said, "If He has everything under His control, He really has it in a mess." But don't blame God; He doesn't have everything on earth under His control. He does, however, have an overall control of the end results.

God has prophesied from the beginning what the end will be, and you can mark it down; it's going to turn out that way! But in the interim, until the lease expires, it is up to mankind to exercise control over the works of the devil here on earth.

God's people have been given authority to pray and intercede for our nation. We must get direction from God, then we must vote godly people into office. If we don't vote godly people into our government, the ungodly fill the positions. We must exercise our rights on earth.

In the fourth chapter of Ephesians, Paul tells us that Jesus has given gifts to men:

> **And he gave some, apostles; and some, prophets; and some, evangelists; and some, pastors and teachers;**
>
> **For the perfecting of the saints, for the work of the ministry, for the edifying of the body of Christ:**
>
> **Till we all come in the unity of the faith, and of the knowledge of the Son of God, unto a perfect man, unto the measure of the stature of the fulness of Christ.**
>
> **Ephesians 4:11-13**

We will never come into the unity of doctrine, but it's possible for Christians to come into unity of faith. Christians should unite in faith for a common cause: to undo the works the devil has done in our nation and our government. It can be done by prayer and voting godly people into government positions. Don't leave it all up to God and then complain when the wicked control the government.

Jesus—our Intercessor, our Advocate—will, by the Holy Spirit, give direction in these matters. God's Spirit knows all things, and if we tune in to the Spirit of God, He will reveal to us what we need to know. (John 16:13.)

No, we are not going into a utopia, where everybody gets better and better. On the contrary, the world is going to become more wicked and more confused, because their darkness is becoming darker. But to believers who walk in light of the Word of God, our light is becoming brighter.

As the wicked come closer to the end, they are coming closer to the kingdom of darkness, so their darkness grows darker.

> **The way of the wicked is as darkness: they know not at what they stumble.**
>
> **Proverbs 4:19**

But as believers we are *coming closer to the kingdom of light,* and *our light is growing lighter.*

> **But the path of the just is as the shining light, that shineth more and more unto the perfect day.**
>
> **Proverbs 4:18**

> **Then spake Jesus again unto them, saying, I am the light of the world: he that followeth me shall not walk in darkness, but shall have the light of life.**
>
> **John 8:12**

The wisdom of God will lead us and guide us with great light in the end time.

A Body Prepared

The Body of Christ on earth has *spiritual authority* here. If we allow demons and evil spirits to destroy our freedom, it is not God's fault. He prepared a body of believers to do the work of God. No, God doesn't have everything under control on the earth, but He has an overall control of the end results.

As Jesus says in Matthew 16:19, "...whatsoever thou shalt bind on earth shall be bound in heaven: and whatsoever thou shalt loose on earth shall be loosed in heaven."

Another rendering of this is, whatever you have authority to bind on earth is what is already bound out of heaven. Stop and ask yourself, "What is it that's bound out of heaven?" Sickness, disease, poverty, all things that hurt and destroy are bound out of heaven!

As the Body of Christ we live with authority on this earth. It was delivered to us by the Lord Jesus Christ. (Matt. 28:18-20; Mark 16:15-20.) So the things on earth are not God's responsibility but our responsibility until the earth lease expires.

Another example is found in the Old Testament where God speaks through the prophet and says, "...take up a lamentation upon" (or against) "the king of Tyrus" (Ezek. 28:12). The king of Tyrus was a man, of course, but some of the things used in describing the king of Tyrus could not have been referring to a man.

In this Scripture we have what we call the law of double reference. It is evident from the Scripture that the king of Tyrus was under the control of a spirit being in the atmosphere above the earth. It wasn't just the physical king of Tyrus but the spiritual wickedness of principalities that controlled him. Remember Paul said:

We wrestle not against flesh and blood, but against principalities, against powers, against the rulers of the darkness of this world, against spiritual wickedness in high places.

Ephesians 6:12

Paul also admonishes us to put on God's armor:

Wherefore take unto you the whole armour of God, that ye may be able to withstand in the evil day, and having done all, to stand.

Ephesians 6:13

Once you have put on God's armor, don't pull it off!

Stand therefore, having your loins girt about with truth....

Ephesians 6:14

The *girt,* which was about the loins, was *the belt* that held the armor, as well as the sword, in place. If there ever was a time we needed to gird ourselves with the Truth, it is today.

People sometimes back off of the Word of God because of something they have experienced. It is a dangerous thing to believe in experience rather than God's Word.

Regardless of what you experience in life, *it does not change God's Word!*

This is also true in the area of intercession. There are some strange things being taught about intercession, and some of it has come about because of someone's personal experience. But we are on dangerous ground when we begin to teach experience that doesn't agree with God's Word.

Putting on prayer armor is something that you do. *You gird yourself with truth*—know what you believe and believe what you know. God gave it to you when you were born again. So put it on, and don't let anyone take it off of you.

> **...having on the breastplate of righteousness;**
>
> **And your feet shod with the preparation of the gospel of peace;**
>
> **Above all, taking the shield of faith, wherewith ye shall be able to quench all the fiery darts of the wicked.**
>
> **And take the helmet of salvation, and the sword of the Spirit, which is the word of God:**
>
> **Praying always with all prayer and supplication in the Spirit....**
>
> **Ephesians 6:14-18**

Here is the way I read this Scripture: "Take the helmet of salvation and the Sword of the Spirit, which is the Word of God, praying always, with all prayer and supplication in the Spirit."

I believe the apostle Paul is referring here to the same thing he is talking about in 1 Corinthians 14:15 where he says, "I will pray with the spirit, and I will pray with the understanding also." He is referring to praying in tongues.

He says, "Take...the sword of the Spirit, which is the word of God praying always..." (Eph. 6:17,18). The Sword of the Spirit is the Word of God *proceeding out of your mouth.* It is *not* a sword *until it comes out of your mouth.* (Rev. 1:16; 2 Thess. 2:8.) I believe it becomes the Sword of the Spirit when your spirit, by the Holy Spirit, prays the Word of God.

I believe when you pray in the Spirit you are praying *the Word of God,* which is the will of God. Your spirit, by the Holy Spirit, is praying *exactly what God's Word says about the situation* for which you are praying.

The apostle Paul said in Romans 8:26:

...for we know not what we should pray for as we ought: but *the Spirit* itself maketh intercession for us with groanings which cannot be uttered.

Jesus, our Intercessor, by the Holy Spirit "maketh intercession for us," even when we don't know how or what to pray. His intercession for us is according to God's Word.

Then in Romans 8:27 Paul says:

...he maketh intercession for the saints according to the will of God.

We saw in a previous chapter that this phrase "the will of" was added by the translator. So this Scripture really says, "He maketh intercession *according to God.*" In other words, He prays the same way God would pray if He prayed about the situation.

You could also be inspired by the Holy Spirit to pray God's Word in your own language. As Paul said, "I will pray with the spirit, and I will pray with the understanding also" (1 Cor. 14:15).

Praying God's Word opens up a way for God's will in the earth.

The Holy Spirit Knows the Answer

Anytime you go to God with a question, His answer will always be in agreement with His Word concerning that matter. When you ask Him about any situation you face, He will remind you of what He has already said in His Word. If God were to pray, He would pray His will, which has already been stated in His Word of Promise. His Word is His will concerning you and your situation.

Several years ago a man said to me, "We are really having financial problems. Would you pray with me?" I didn't know how to pray, because I really didn't know his situation, so I began to pray in tongues.

As I was praying, some words came up in my spirit, and I heard this: "He has eaten his seed. He is in such bad financial condition that he is not giving. He is not getting a harvest because he is not planting." (Any farmer knows that when you eat your seed you are in trouble!)

The Spirit of God spoke up on the inside of me and said: "Give him a hundred dollars and tell him not to spend it on himself, but to give it away. Tell him it is seed money."

When I gave him the money and told him he was to give it away, he said the Lord had already spoken to him about giving fifty dollars to two different ministries. Then he said, "But I spent the money and didn't have anything to give."

Three months later when I saw him, he told me he had done as God had directed him and had given fifty dollars to two different ministries. As a result, his wife had gotten a job, he had gotten a raise, and all their bills had been paid! He planted in faith, and the seed produced after its kind.

Trusting the Holy Spirit

A friend of mine had a ministry of helping drug addicts to get off drugs. There were so many of them coming to his house every week for a Bible study that the police thought he was selling drugs.

One of the converts, who had been born again at his Bible study, called him and said, "Could you come over here to my apartment? I need to talk to you. I really have a problem and don't know what to do!"

So my friend went over to see him. When he arrived at the apartment, he found the problem: it was full of stolen merchandise.

The new convert said, "What am I going to do? I was spaced out on drugs when I stole this stuff. I can't take it back. I don't know where it came from—and if I did, they would put me in jail. And I'm a changed man! But what am I going to do?"

The first thought that came into my friend's mind was Romans 8:26: "...for we know not what we should pray for as we ought: but the Spirit itself maketh intercession for us with groanings which cannot be uttered." So he said, "Let's pray in the Spirit." They both prayed in tongues until they felt a release in their spirits, then he went home.

In a few days the new convert called, all excited. He said, "You can't believe what happened. I went out for two or three hours, and when I came back somebody had broken in and taken *all that stolen merchandise!*"

When you have a problem and there seems to be no answer, God's Spirit knows the answer. (No, God doesn't condone theft, but that thief was going to steal from somebody.) There is *nothing* impossible with God, and all things are possible to those that believe.

The Bible says of Abraham that when there was no hope he believed in hope. (Rom. 4:18.) *You* may be saying, "There's no hope for me financially." Don't say that any longer! Go to the Word of God and get some supernatural hope. God's Word is the answer to your problem. I can't tell you exactly what that answer is, but the Spirit of God knows how to pray concerning your situation.

Spend time praying in the Spirit every day. Remember, the Spirit of Truth will teach you and guide you into all truth. He will show you things to come and how to pray as God would pray. (John 16:13; Rom. 8:26-28.)

Praying Beyond Your Ability

Tom Underhill, who is a personal friend of mine and pastor of Russellville Christian Center in Russellville, Arkansas, gave this testimony of an experience he had praying in the Spirit over an accident victim.

Several years ago on a hot summer day, he was driving on Interstate 40 from Little Rock to his home in Russellville, and traffic was thick. As he topped a hill west of Conway, he saw an accident that had just taken place on a bridge.

When he got close enough, he could see that a Ford Thunderbird had run under the back end of a truck loaded with sod. There were women lying on the roadway, and it appeared they were injured severely. So he stopped, went over to the ladies, and began to try to comfort them.

He noticed that one of them, who looked to be in her forties, was hurt badly and seemed to be unconscious. He held her head in his lap and began to pray in tongues. He prayed for her by the help of the Holy Spirit until medical help came. After all the victims were transported to hospitals, he drove on home, with no thought of ever seeing that lady again.

The Russellville Christian Center has had many people accept Jesus as their Lord and Savior each year. Most of the time they have had no previous contact with these people.

But about a year after this accident, Tom and his wife, Bonnie, were visiting with a new convert. She began to tell about an accident she was involved in sometime before. As she described the accident, Tom realized that she was the one he had held that day and prayed for until the ambulance came.

They all got excited as they realized that Jesus, the Intercessor, by the Holy Spirit, had prayed the perfect prayer through Tom, when he did not know how to in that situation. And all that he prayed about in the Spirit worked together for good.

Tom said, "I know now that the Holy Spirit prayed through my spirit for that woman to live, and be healed and born again. Praise God! God even sent her to my church to make that decision."

Praying in the Spirit allows Jesus, the Intercessor, to flow through you. As the Word says, "...pray one for that ye may be healed" (James 5:16). Make a channel through which the Holy Spirit can minister to others. Give Jesus liberty to intercede through you in behalf of others, for He prays the way God would pray.

Spiritual Communication Lost

In the garden Adam walked and talked with God in the cool of the day. (Gen. 3:8.) God is a Spirit, and there was a *spiritual* communication between God and Adam. Until Adam sinned, his tongue was connected to his spirit. I believe that connection severed or shorted out because of sin. He then began to be ruled by his carnal mind. He had lost control of his tongue.

James said:

> **And the tongue is a fire, a world of iniquity: so is the tongue among our members, that it defileth the whole body, and setteth on fire the course of nature; and it is set on fire of hell.**
>
> **For every kind of beasts, and of birds, and of serpents, and of things in the sea, is tamed, and hath been tamed of mankind:**
>
> **But the tongue can no man tame; it is an unruly evil, full of deadly poison.**
>
> **James 3:6-8**

We know that God didn't set man's tongue on fire of hell! Satan, the deceiver, poisoned man's tongue through deception. His tongue was then dominated by his flesh instead of his spirit.

Communication Restored

When we are born again, we become a new creature in Christ Jesus. When we are baptized in the Holy Spirit, as in Acts 2:4, *we get our tongue hooked up to our spirit again.*

Then we are able to communicate with our Father in the Spirit. Every word you speak from the time you learn to talk comes out of your head (your thought pattern) until you are baptized in the Holy Spirit and speak with other tongues. Then as you pray in the Spirit, that language comes up out of your spirit rather than your head. That is why it is referred to as speaking in other tongues.

God wants us to worship Him in Spirit and in truth. (John 4:23.) Certainly people who have not received the Holy Spirit baptism can worship God! But there is a spiritual communication through tongues, a flow of the Spirit of God like a river that never dries up. It is a refreshing that is supernatural. (Isa. 28:11,12.)

The promise is for "all that are afar off, even as many as the Lord our God shall call" (Acts 2:39). In the sixteenth chapter of Mark, Jesus said, "These signs shall follow them that believe...." Then one of the signs He mentioned was: "In my name... they shall speak with new tongues" (v. 17). Every believer has the right to speak with new tongues.

You may have grown up in a church where they taught that speaking in tongues went out with the apostles. You may even have been taught it is of the devil. But we find in Acts 2:4 that speaking in tongues was of God; in Acts 8 it was of God; in Acts 10 it was of God; in Acts 19 it was of God. *It is still of God today!*

I heard of a gambler who went with a minister to a Full Gospel Businessmen's meeting, where people were speaking in tongues as they were baptized in the Holy Spirit.

On the way home that night the minister, who didn't believe in speaking in tongues, said to the gambler, "Don't you get mixed up with those folks. That tongues business is of the devil!"

The gambler replied, "Now, preacher, I've served the devil for forty years, and I've been in every bar and dive in this town. If speaking in tongues was of the devil, I'd surely have been speaking in tongues a long time ago!"

Speaking in tongues was of God in Paul's day, and it is still of God today. Yet, I realize the devil tries to produce a counterfeit. But don't throw the baby out with the bath water, so to speak.

Remember Jesus' words: "The Comforter, which is the Holy Ghost, whom the Father will send in my name, he shall teach you all things.... When he, the Spirit of truth, is come, he will guide you into all truth" (John 14:26; 16:13). Thank God, the Comforter has come!

Paul put it this way:

(For the weapons of our warfare are not carnal, but mighty through God to the puling down of strong holds;)

Casting down imaginations, and every high thing that exalteth itself against the knowledge of God, and bringing into captivity every thought to the obedience of Christ.

2 Corinthians 10:4,5

Praying in the Spirit (in tongues) is a supernatural way of casting down wrong imaginations and bringing every thought into obedience to Christ. Man cannot tame the tongue with his own ability, but the Holy Spirit is capable of taming the tongue.

10

Following the Spirit
in Prayer

10

Following the Spirit in Prayer

Follow after charity, and desire spiritual gifts, but rather that ye may prophesy.

For he that speaketh in an unknown tongue speaketh not unto men, but unto God: for no man understandeth him; howbeit in the spirit he speaketh mysteries.

1 Corinthians 14:1,2

Here is verse 2 from *The Amplified Bible:*

For one who speaks in an [unknown] tongue speaks not to men but to God, for no one understands or catches his meaning, because in the [Holy] Spirit he utters secret truths and hidden things [not obvious to the understanding].

We could say the ability to communicate secret truths of God the Father is one of the weapons of our warfare. This is not the only weapon, but it is a supernatural weapon available to every believer.

He that speaketh in an unknown tongue edifieth himself, but he that prophesieth edifieth the church.

1 Corinthians 14:4

Paul goes on to say:

I would...rather that ye prophesied...that the church may receive edifying.

1 Corinthians 14:5

The word *edify* means to build up,[1] like you would charge a battery. Your spirit is designed of God to receive and communicate with God the Father. Notice again Paul's statement: "He that speaketh in an unknown tongue speaketh not unto men, but unto God...howbeit in the spirit he speaketh mysteries." When you speak in an unknown tongue (unknown to the one doing the speaking), you are speaking mysteries, which you do not understand. But your spirit is communicating directly with God, uttering secret truths, praying God's Word in a manner which you have not understood with your carnal mind. You are in perfect agreement with God and His will concerning the matter for which you are praying.

For if I pray in an unknown tongue, my spirit prayeth, but my understanding is unfruitful.

What is it then? I will pray with the spirit, and I will pray with the understanding also: I will sing

---

[1] James H. Strong, *Strong's Exhaustive Concordance* (Grand Rapids: Baker Book House, 1992), "Greek Dictionary of the New Testament," p. 51, #3618.

with the spirit, and I will sing with the under-standing also.

1 Corinthians 14:14,15

In other words, Paul was saying, "I will do it both ways." Praying in the Spirit is a supernatural communication with our Father God.

James said the tongue is an unruly evil, full of deadly poison; it is set on fire of hell, and no man can tame it. (James 3:6-8.) Some might say if no man can tame it, then it's a hopeless situation. But as you study the context of James's statement, you will realize he is referring to the fact that the tongue cannot be tamed with man's natural ability. Yet, it is not hopeless; the supernatural power of the Holy Spirit can tame the tongue.

When Adam sinned, he lost the supernatural link to his spirit, and his tongue was then controlled by his carnal mind. His head ruled his tongue. But when we receive the Holy Spirit baptism, God's Spirit flows through our spirit, and the tongue is connected again to the human spirit.

Supernatural Prayer

We are capable then of speaking out of our spirit, by inspiration of the Holy Spirit, mysteries, secret truths, and things not obvious to the understanding. When we are praying in tongues, we are praying the way God prays, and Satan can't prevail against it. This is the Sword of the Spirit and praying the Word of God supernaturally.

Paul talks about this in Romans 8:26 where he says we don't know how to pray as we ought, then the Spirit helps our infirmities. He helps our weaknesses and makes intercession for us with groanings which cannot be uttered in articulate speech, or in a language we know.

Then in verse 28 Paul says, "And we know that all things work together for good to them that love God, to them who are the called according to his purpose." What is going to "work together for good"? *All things that we prayed about in the Spirit.*

Jesus is seated at the right hand of the Father. He is there to make intercession for us, yet He does it through His Body here on earth. When you have an urge to pray for someone and have no knowledge of that person's situation, by praying in the Spirit you are allowing Jesus to pray through you in the perfect will of God concerning that matter. Yet your understanding will be unfruitful, unless He gives you revelation or interpretation of what you are praying.

Revelation by the Holy Spirit

As Paul said, "If I pray in an unknown tongue, my spirit prayeth, but my understanding is unfruitful" (1 Cor. 14:14). You don't have to know what you are praying about in the Spirit, for you trust the Intercessor, and you know you are praying the perfect will of God concerning that matter. The more you pray in the Spirit, the more sensitive you become to the direction of the Holy Spirit.

Supernatural Revelation

While one minister was praying in the Spirit, alone in his church, he saw into the spirit realm, and there was an evil spirit hovering over the church. He commanded that spirit to come down and leave his church in Jesus' Name—and it left immediately. The spiritual atmosphere of that church changed overnight.

That revelation came through the discerning of spirits. We should never lose a battle in the realm of the spirit. The human spirit is much more sensitive to God-given revelation than the carnal mind.

Paul said:

> **...Eye hath not seen, nor ear heard, neither have entered into the heart of man, the things which God hath prepared for them that love him.**
>
> **But God hath revealed them unto us by his Spirit: for the Spirit searcheth all things, yea, the deep things of God.**
>
> 1 Corinthians 2:9,10

This is the way God gives revelation: by His Spirit into your spirit. But if you are locked into the carnal realm, you will never get this kind of revelation. Our physical eyes have not seen, our physical ears have not heard, and it hasn't entered into our hearts through the five physical senses. Yet the revelation is transferred by God's Spirit into our spirit.

You will notice in the *King James Version* that in "revealed unto us by his Spirit," the word *Spirit* is capitalized, for it is speaking of the Holy Spirit. But in the next phrase, "for the Spirit searcheth," the word *spirit* should not be capitalized for it is referring to the human spirit.

The Holy Spirit doesn't need to search the things of God, for He already knows the deep things of God. It is the *human spirit* that searches for the deep things of God.

> **For what man knoweth the things of a man, save the spirit of man which is in him?**
>
> **1 Corinthians 2:11**

Your (human) spirit knows all about you, much more than you know in your head.

Since your spirit knows all about you, and God's Spirit knows all about God, when you get these two in communication with each other, you have tapped the Source of all knowledge.

This doesn't mean you have all knowledge, but you have tapped the Source of all knowledge. You are capable of drawing from the Spirit of God the truth about any situation you may face in life.

> **Now we have received, not the spirit of the world, but the spirit which is of God; that we might know the things that are freely given to us of God.**
>
> **1 Corinthians 2:12**

This is referring to the human spirit.

The human spirit is designed of God to pick up things that our natural mind cannot perceive. This perception comes by revelation. God, by His Holy Spirit, reveals it to your spirit.

God's Spirit through your spirit reveals truth and understanding which you could not receive through your five physical senses. If you will learn to draw from that anointing, He will reveal what you need to know about any situations or circumstances you may face in life. (John 16:13-15; James 1:5-7.)

There will be times when you will have *no idea* how you know, but you will know that you know, and you know it *by the Spirit* of God. This is a revelation of the Spirit of God into the human spirit.

A look at Genesis 2:7 will give us some insight concerning this matter: "And the Lord God formed man of the dust of the ground, and breathed into his nostrils the breath of life." (The *Amplified Bible* says "the spirit of life.") Notice God *formed* Adam's body. He didn't create it; He *formed* it. He took something He had already created and then molded (made) a physical body. The next thing He did was to breathe His Spirit life into that body.

If God breathed His Spirit life into Adam, it was the Spirit of God. Adam's human spirit came from God, who is a Spirit. Therefore, he was capable of fellowshiping and communicating with God through his spirit.

The bad news is: when Adam disobeyed God, that communion link of their spirits was disconnected.

The good news is: when you are born again, God restores the capability of the receiver inside you so that you can receive from God revelation and understanding concerning His promises.

Sometimes I have heard people say, "The devil told me this or that—and by the way, do you have a word for me?" *It's amazing* that they can tell me what the devil said, but they want to know if I have a word from the Lord for them! They should be able to hear God more easily than they can hear the devil. Their spirits were designed to pick up on what God is saying rather than what the devil is saying. But the problem is that their spirits are more in tune with carnality than with the Spirit of God.

The more you pray in the Spirit (in tongues), the more sensitive you will become to the Spirit of God and what He is saying. The more you quote the devil, the more sensitive you will become to what he is saying through your carnal mind.

The key is to get your receiver (spirit) tuned to God's frequency, by quoting God's Word and speaking what He has said about you. Then you will become highly developed in hearing His voice in your spirit. Your spirit knows all about you, and God's Spirit knows all about God. So when you link your spirit and God's Spirit together, that's a winning combination any way you look at it.

Let's read verse 12 again from 1 Corinthians, chapter 2, and add two more verses:

Now we have received, not the spirit of the world, but the spirit which is of God; that we might know the things that are freely given to us of God.

Which things also we speak, not in the words which man's wisdom teacheth, but which the Holy Ghost teacheth; comparing spiritual things with spiritual.

But the natural man receiveth not the things of the Spirit of God: for they are foolishness unto him: neither can he know them, because they are spiritually discerned.

1 Corinthians 2:12-14

There are two or three ways you could look at these verses. The words *natural man* could refer to the man who is not born again; he does not normally receive the things of the Spirit of God. I am convinced it is also referring to the physical man. The natural body does not receive the things of the Spirit of God. You can't touch God with your physical body.

Everything you receive from God comes first into your human spirit. The human spirit is the reception center of all that God gives. Whether it is divine healing, the baptism of the Holy Spirit, or salvation, it must first be received into the human spirit. You must conceive it in your spirit, then it is manifested outwardly in your body.

This is why it is so important that we don't always go by our feelings. We are to walk by faith and not by sight. (2 Cor. 5:7.) If you go by your feelings, you are going to wait until you *feel* healed before you *believe* you are healed, or you are going to wait until you *feel* saved before you *believe* you are saved. But God doesn't do any credit business; you must have faith up front—faith *before you receive,* not after. (Mark 11:23,24; Rom. 10:8-10.)

God wants us to receive through our spirit by faith. That is why people have trouble receiving the baptism of the Holy Spirit and speaking with other tongues. They want to wait until they can see or hear a manifestation before they will believe.

But tongues is a result of the infilling of the Holy Spirit. We receive the Holy Spirit because we believe and act on the Word of Promise. How could you speak in tongues before you believe you have received? How could you be healed before you believe? Somebody said, "I'll believe I'm healed when I *feel* like it." Why in the world would you want to believe it then? That wouldn't take any faith at all, because it would be in the realm of knowledge.

When you conceive it in your spirit, then it will manifest itself in your physical body. Remember, *the human spirit is the reception center of all God has given you!*

> **But the natural man receiveth not the things of the Spirit of God: for they are foolishness unto him: neither can he know them, because they are spiritually discerned.**
>
> **But he that is spiritual judgeth all things....**
>
> **1 Corinthians 2:14,15**

Who is he that is spiritual? The inner man, *your spirit,* is the spiritual part of you. Your spirit judges all things, but no man can judge your spirit. People may judge your actions, but they can't judge your spirit. Yet the Holy Spirit is able to reveal the thoughts and intents of man's heart to your spirit.

A Direct-Line Communication

When you receive the Holy Spirit baptism, you are capable of becoming a direct line in the spirit through which Jesus is able to make intercession for people and nations here on earth.

Jesus is seated at the right hand of the Father, yet He has a legal right to make intercession through your voice here on earth, for you are a legal resident of this planet.

For who hath known the mind of the Lord, that he may instruct him? But we have the mind of Christ.
1 Corinthians 2:16

What a statement! "We have the mind of Christ." Jesus Christ is our Intercessor. He is our Advocate. He is our Lawyer, so to speak, representing us before the Father.

Jesus, Our Advocate

If you have missed it and you are condemned by the devil, 1 John 1:9 is good news: "If we confess our sins, he is faithful and just to forgive us our sins, and to cleanse us from all unrighteousness." Acting on that will stop Satan in his tracks. But you must believe and act on it in faith.

I have heard some Christians say, "I confessed my sin, but I don't feel any better."

What does feeling have to do with it? Your feelings won't change God's Word. But if you believe and hold fast to the Word of God, your feelings will change. Sometimes your feelings will fail you, *but the Word of God will never fail you!* When you become fully persuaded that God's Word is true, your feelings will begin to line up with His Word.

Look at It This Way

So you missed it. The Word says God is the Judge, and Jesus is your Advocate. So look at it this way: your Father is the Judge and your Brother is your Lawyer, and the devil doesn't have a chance if you have repented and have forsaken your sin.

What shall we then say to these things? If God be for us, who can be against us?

He that spared not his own Son, but delivered him up for us all, how shall he not with him also freely give us all things?

Who shall lay any thing to the charge of God's elect? It is God that justifieth.

Who is he that condemneth? It is Christ that died, yea rather, that is risen again, who is even at the right hand of God, who also maketh intercession for us.

Romans 8:31-34

Jesus as your Advocate is on your side. He intercedes for you.

Most people think God is mad at them because of their sin. But God is love. He wants you to confess and forsake your sins so that Jesus can represent you before Him. When Jesus represents you before the Father, the Father sees you through the blood of Jesus. He sees His righteousness in you.

> **For he [God] hath made him [Jesus] to be sin for us, who knew no sin; that we might be made the righteousness of God in him.**
>
> **2 Corinthians 5:21**

Can we fathom the depths of such a statement? "...that we might be made the righteousness of God in him." Not our own righteousness, but His.

One With Him

Look at the words of Jesus in John's gospel as He prayed to His Father God:

> **I have given them thy word; and the world hath hated them, because they are not of the world, even as I am not of the world.**
>
> **I pray not that thou shouldest take them out of the world, but that thou shouldest keep them from the evil.**
>
> **They are not of the world, even as I am not of the world.**

Sanctify them through thy truth: thy word is truth. As thou hast sent me into the world, even so have I also sent them into the world.

And for their sakes I sanctify myself, that they also might be sanctified through the truth.

Neither pray I for these alone, but for them also which shall believe on me through their word;

That they all may be one; as thou, Father, art in me, and I in thee, that they also may be one in us: that the world may believe that thou hast sent me.

And the glory which thou gayest me I have given them; that they may be one, even as we are one.

John 17:14-22

As God sent Jesus into the world, *even so,* Jesus has sent us. *And the glory which God gave Him, He has given to us, that we might be one.* Jesus was talking about all believers.

Remember the Scripture phrase in Hebrews 10:5, "...a body hast thou prepared me." There is no doubt this Scripture has a dual meaning. In one sense it refers to the physical body of Jesus that was given as a sin offering. But God has also prepared Him a Body that is physically on earth today to represent Him here, while He is in heaven. Jesus is seated at the right hand of God the Father. Yet He still has a Body functioning in the earth today. *The Body of Christ is alive and well on the planet Earth.* It is the only Body Jesus has to work through on the earth today. His present-day intercessory ministry must be channeled through His Body here on earth.

In Colossians, the apostle Paul makes these profound statements:

> Who now rejoice in my sufferings for you, and fill up that which is behind of the afflictions of Christ in my flesh for his body's sake, which is the church:
>
> Whereof I am made a minister, according to the dispensation of God which is given to me for you, to fulfil the word of God;
>
> To whom God would make known what is the riches of the glory of this mystery among the Gentiles; which is Christ in you, the hope of glory.
>
> Colossians 1:24,25,27

God's hope for this planet is "Christ in you," Christ working through His Body on earth today. The Body which God has prepared on earth is the Body of Christ. The world has been reconciled and restored to favor with God through what Christ did in their behalf. But they don't know about it and have not received Christ as their Savior. So God has given us the ministry of reconciliation.

The *Amplified Bible* puts it like this:

> It was God [personally present] in Christ, reconciling and restoring the world to favor with Himself, not counting up and holding against [men] their trespasses [but cancelling them], and committing to us the message of reconciliation (of the restoration to favor).
>
> So we are Christ's ambassadors, God making His appeal as it were through us. We [as Christ's

personal representatives] beg you for His sake to lay hold of the divine favor [now offered you] and be reconciled to God.

2 Corinthians 5:19,20

It seems that the intercessory ministry of Jesus is limited to what the Body of Christ will let Him do through that Body. We are not really the intercessors, but we are His agents here on earth. *He is the Intercessor.* But for Jesus to effectively carry out His present-day ministry of intercession, His Body on earth must respond by allowing Him to intercede through them the way God would pray.

That supernatural flow *will never fail!* However, imperfect vessels sometimes fail to yield to the Intercessor. Christ has a Body through which He can exercise authority in the earth today to the degree that they will respond to His intercession.

I have declared unto them thy name, and will declare it: that the love wherewith thou hast loved me may be in them, and I in them.

John 17:26

For Jesus to fulfill His declaration, He must declare it through His Body that is here on earth. Jesus now has a glorified body and is seated at the right hand of the Father. He has been restored to His divine power and glory that He once had with the Father. (John 17:5.) He is as much God as God is God, for They are One.

Yet because you are a member of the Body of Christ and serve as His agent here on earth, Jesus can legally intercede by way of the Holy Spirit through your spirit in a supernatural language, praying the perfect will of God. Then you know that heaven, earth, and all hell will stand at attention, for He prays the way God would pray.

We could say it this way: Christ in us—the hope of glory—until the lease expires and He returns in the clouds to receive us unto Himself.

So we dare not limit His ministry, but allow Him to intercede through us to exercise dominion in the earth, thereby declaring His Name, His power, and His glory.

Prayer of Salvation

God loves you—no matter who you are, no matter what your past. God loves you so much that He gave His one and only begotten Son for you. The Bible tells us that "...whoever believes in him shall not perish but have eternal life" (John 3:16 NIV). Jesus laid down His life and rose again so that we could spend eternity with Him in heaven and experience His absolute best on earth. If you would like to receive Jesus into your life, say the following prayer out loud and mean it from your heart.

Heavenly Father, I come to You admitting that I am a sinner. Right now, I choose to turn away from sin, and I ask You to cleanse me of all unrighteousness. I believe that Your Son, Jesus, died on the cross to take away my sins. I also believe that He rose again from the dead so that I might be forgiven of my sins and made righteous through faith in Him. I call upon the name of Jesus Christ to be the Savior and Lord of my life. Jesus, I choose to follow You and ask that You fill me with the power of the Holy Spirit. I declare that right now I am a child of God. I am free from sin and full of the righteousness of God. I am saved in Jesus' name. Amen.

If you prayed this prayer to receive Jesus Christ as your Savior for the first time, please contact us on the Web at **www.harrisonhouse.com** to receive a free book.

Or you may write to us at:

Harrison House
P.O. Box 35035
Tulsa, Oklahoma 74153

About the Author

Charles Capps is a retired farmer, land developer, and ordained minister who travels throughout the United States sharing the truth of God's Word. He has taught Bible seminars for twenty-four years sharing how Christians can apply the Word to the circumstances of life and live victoriously.

In the mid '90s the Lord gave Charles an assignment to teach end-time events and a revelation of the coming of the Lord.

Besides authoring several books, including the best-selling *The Tongue, A Creative Force,* and the minibook *God's Creative Power,* which has sold over 3 million copies, Charles Capps Ministries has a national daily syndicated radio broadcast called "Concepts of Faith."

For a complete list of books and tapes
by Charles Capps, write:

Charles Capps Ministries
P.O. Box 69
England, AR 72046

Or visit him on the Web at:
www.charlescapps.com

Powerful Teaching From Charles Capps

If you've enjoyed the *When Jesus Prays Through You,* you can find more dynamic teaching from Charles Capps in these revolutionary books.

You Have Authority in Christ

Your Spiritual Authority

Charles Capps shares a penetrating message on the believer's legal right to exercise authority in the earth today. This dele-

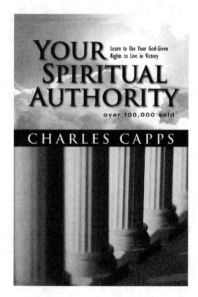

gated authority was given to every Christian so that the sick can be healed, finances can be loosed, and those bound by Satan may be free. You will learn that you have dominion through your words, that your body gives you authority on the earth, that being born of the Spirit gives you the ability to use Jesus' name, and many other powerful principles.

ISBN: 1-57794-668-5

Discover the Source of Lasting Success

Success Motivation

Discover the one way to achieve true and lasting success. It's found through the Word of God. The image that God's Word builds inside you can become the most powerful force in your life. That image causes you to succeed when others fail. It is spiritual motivation to the human spirit, and it will bring you success in every part of your life spiritually, physically, financially, and socially.

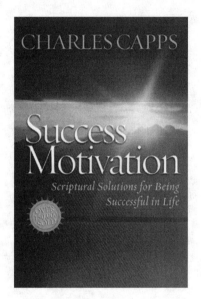

ISBN: 1-57794-667-7

Available at fine bookstores everywhere
or at **www.harrisonhouse.com**.

Uncover God's System for Answered Prayer

Releasing the Ability of God Through Prayer

God's Word is alive and powerful! It is living substance. When you learn to pray in line with God's Word, you release the ability of God and bring Him on the scene in your behalf. Discover the power of prayer that is governed by spiritual laws and designed to work for you. It is more powerful than the laws of nature that rule the universe today.

ISBN: 1-57794-669-3

Available at fine bookstores everywhere or at **www.harrisonhouse.com**.

Speak Life and Live Better, Stronger and Longer!

Join the millions whose lives have been changed by the *God's Creative Power Series*. This dynamic series from Charles Capps has sold over 5 million copies. Each book reveals powerful teaching on the power of your words and includes scriptural confessions that will change the way you think and the way you live.

God's Creative Power Will Work for You— Over 3 Million Sold!

Charles Capps' original mini-book reveals that the power of the spoken word can change your destiny. God created the universe by speaking it into existence. He has given the same ability to you through your words. To be effective in life, you must speak words of faith. Let faith-filled words put you over!

ISBN 0-89274-024-8

God's Creative Power for Healing— Over 1.5 Million Sold!

This powerful book combines all new teaching with Scripture confessions for healing. You will learn how you can release the ability of God for your healing with the words of your mouth.

ISBN 0-89274-815-X

www.harrisonhouse.com

Fast. Easy. Convenient!

- ◆ New Book Information
- ◆ Look Inside the Book
- ◆ Press Releases
- ◆ Bestsellers

- ◆ Free E-News
- ◆ Author Biographies
- ◆ Upcoming Books
- ◆ Share Your Testimony

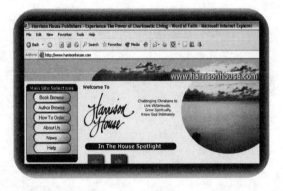

For the latest in book news and author information, please visit us on the Web at www.harrisonhouse.com. Get up-to-date pictures and details on all our powerful and life-changing products. Sign up for our e-mail newsletter, *Friends of the House,* and receive free monthly information on our authors and products including testimonials, author announcements, and more!

Harrison House—
Books That Bring Hope, Books That Bring Change

The Harrison House Vision

Proclaiming the truth and the power

Of the Gospel of Jesus Christ

With excellence;

Challenging Christians to

Live victoriously,

Grow spiritually,

Know God intimately.